T0348109

YOUR LIFE,
MATTERS

PETREA KING

YOUR LIFE, MATTERS

The Power of Living Now

RANDOM HOUSE AUSTRALIA

Every effort has been made to acknowledge and contact the owners of copyright for permission to reproduce material which falls under the 1968 Copyright Act. Any copyright owners who have inadvertently been omitted from acknowledgements and credits should contact the publisher and omissions will be rectified in subsequent editions.

Random House Australia Pty Ltd
Level 3, 100 Pacific Highway, North Sydney, NSW 2060
http://www.randomhouse.com.au

Sydney   New York   Toronto
London   Auckland   Johannesburg

First published by Random House Australia in 2004
This edition first published by Random House Australia in 2005

Copyright © Petrea King 2004

All rights reserved. No part of this publication may be reproduced, stored in a retrieval system, or transmitted in any form or by any means, electronic, mechanical, photocopying, recording or otherwise, without the prior written permission of the publisher.

National Library of Australia
Cataloguing-in-Publication Entry

King, Petrea, 1951- .
Your life matters: the power of living now.

ISBN 978 1 74051 363 0.
ISBN 1 74051 363 0.

1. Self-realization. 2. Peace of mind. 3. Contentment. I. Title.

155.2

Cover illustration by Adrian Cook
Cover and internal design by saso content and design
Typeset by Midland Typesetters, Maryborough, Victoria
Printed and bound by Griffin Press, South Australia

To my many teachers

Author's Note

Throughout this book, I have drawn on examples from my clients and the participants who have attended our residential programs at the Quest for Life Centre. To protect their privacy and ensure confidentiality I have changed people's names and identifying details unless an individual has expressed the desire to own his or her own story. I am grateful to them for their willingness to entrust me with their deepest questions about life and the sacred stories of their lives. In their willingness to share so deeply they have helped me find the words to describe the inner journey we all seem to share. Each has been my saviour and given me boundless love, courage, strength and more.

Contents

Acknowledgements ix

Preface xi

Chapter 1 Welcome to the Planet 1

Chapter 2 What Matters 19

Chapter 3 Peace Matters 38

Chapter 4 Physical Matters 56

Chapter 5 Beliefs Matter 87

Chapter 6 Meditation Matters 134

Chapter 7 Mind Matters 148

Chapter 8 Emotional Matters 175

The Petrea King Quest for Life Centre 228

Petrea King Collection 232

Acknowledgements

It was Aristotle who believed that a physician had to experience a disease before attempting to cure it. I have been a very desperate woman on many occasions and those experiences have pushed me into exploring parts of myself that I'd never have ventured into otherwise. Everything within the covers of this book has been borne out of personal experience. However, I have been blessed with the very best of teachers.

There are simply too many people to thank for this book's gestation – no encounter is a coincidence and every moment is a precious one. Everything that needed to, unfolded so that this book came into being in its own perfect timing.

Half of this book was written two years before I could create the time to complete it. In the intervening time the sheer volume of teaching in many more programs at the Quest for Life Centre, the interviews, lecturing and working with people in particularly challenging situations honed my ability to put these ideas on paper.

My thanks to all those magnificent people who shared their stories with me. You have been my teachers, my friends and my guides. Without you I wouldn't be me.

Amongst all the people who've assisted me in this process, some stand out as shining lights. Thank you to Susan Varga and Anne Coombs who provided a beautiful writing space for the first two weeks of the writing of this book, and to Sonia Williams and Lyn Perkin who opened their hearts, home and larder to provide the perfect writing environment for the last two weeks of its completion. Thanks to you all for the love, laughter and conversation.

To my partner in life, love and every page of this book, Wendie Batho, I give my deepest thanks. She sat by my side and contributed her ideas, humour, quotes and comments, and provided endless cups and plates of whatever was required to physically sustain me. Her greatest gifts to me are her capacity to love unconditionally and to have complete faith in me. She has perfected the art of 'fluffing' someone up and I'm grateful and fortunate to be her chief recipient.

Thanks also to the staff and volunteers at the Quest for Life Centre who endeavour to live the message of this book, and particularly to Thomas-Andrew, who released me from the day-to-day concerns of running an organisation. The existence and work of the Centre is daily proof that, with faith and constancy, seemingly impossible dreams can come true.

My parents, Geoff and Rae, are the most loving and supportive parents anyone could dream of and I thank them for their faith in me.

Thanks also to Wendy Hughes and her son, Scott, who made sense of my scrawled diagrams and to Lucy Tumanov-West who saved you, the reader, from considerable confusion through her skilful editing.

My agent, Mary Cunnane, came into my life at the completion of this book. My thanks to her for her encouragement and practical suggestions about the book's structure.

Preface

Right now we are living in the most challenging, exciting and critical time in our history. We have the capacity to annihilate life on a grand scale and at the very same time, we have the ability to find creative solutions to almost every problem of human existence. Our choices will have profound consequences for human history.

Mother earth will continue with or without our presence so, from the planet's perspective, it makes little difference whether we awaken to the challenge or not. However, once awake, would anyone choose willingly to return to the slumber of ignorance? Your life has consequence, it matters. We each have a role to play in awakening ourselves to the fullness of life and the possibilities that living in the present afford us. Together we can find a more peaceable way of living with others and ourselves.

It seems that it is often an unexpected event that provides the necessary impetus to reflect upon our life, to see what needs to be changed and to begin that process. I have sat with many people in their last hours of life. Some people look back in disappointment at a life they feel they've wasted. Other people talk of their sadness at not having offered forgiveness or that they never told those who were important to them how much they were loved. Some people talk of the regret of not having made a greater contribution in their life. That seems a tragedy to me. I think we would all prefer to look back with peace in our hearts knowing that, even though our life may have brought many unexpected events, we had done our best to meet the challenges we faced.

Imagine a peaceful sanctuary, secluded from the world, set in beautiful countryside, a haven to retreat to, where you can rest and refresh yourself, somewhere to be heard and to discover that what truly ails you can be healed. Imagine a place where people listen to you, where they weep and laugh with you, and share your hopes and fears; where, through gentle, compassionate recognition, you can explore, and accept the events in your life and find your own best answers to your dilemmas.

Such a place exists at the Quest for Life Centre and welcomes to its doors those seeking ways to establish peace and healing in their lives. What precipitates their journey to the Quest for Life Centre varies greatly. People come because they're seeking peace and reconciliation with the events of their lives and to find ways to live more passionately in the present. They come because they are living with suffering and want to find a more peaceable way of being in the midst of unfolding anguish. Some people come because they feel they haven't been living the lives they came here to live; they come to set down baggage that no longer serves them and to find deeper meaning and purpose in their lives. Further information about the Quest for Life Centre and its programs is detailed at the end of this book.

This book has a central theme and it is this: your life matters and your existence is precious; take the opportunity to awaken to your own loving potential and to establish peace in your daily life by developing a living, practical spirituality, based in consciousness.

Forgive me when I have used he, she, him or her in isolation rather than the more clumsy he/she and him/her. Please understand that the ideas I am articulating in this book are beyond concern with the physicality of our differences.

I have endeavoured to make this book an easy read, however there's much in it that requires your active participation and self-reflection. There may be points where you'll want to put the book down and reflect on how the ideas it contains apply to your own life. By all means, take these ideas into your quiet time or meditation for reflection.

I enjoyed writing this book a great deal and was also inspired by doing it. I hope that my enthusiasm will reach out and touch you as you read it.

Petrea King
Founder, Quest for Life Centre

CHAPTER 1

Welcome to the Planet

The purpose of our existence is to seek happiness.

Dalai Lama

Happiness is an inside job.

Me

*Every truth passes through three stages before it is
recognised.
In the first, it is ridiculed.
In the second, it is opposed.
In the third, it is regarded as self-evident.*

Arthur Schopenhauer

*Not in entire forgetfulness,
And not in utter nakedness,
But trailing clouds of glory do we come
From God, who is our home:
Heaven lies about us in our infancy!
Shades of the prison-house begin to close
Upon the growing Boy . . .*

William Wordsworth

We are not human beings with a bit of spirituality tacked on.
Rather, we are consciousness, or vibrating energy, embodied;
our bodies reside within this energetic field. So rather than thinking

of human beings as having a spiritual aspect, secondary to the physical, it is completely the reverse – we are spiritual or vibrating eternal energy first and foremost. Rather than the body having a consciousness, we are consciousness enmeshed in a body. Life changes when this perception is adopted.

We're often aware of the energetic field around people and get a sense of their 'atmosphere' even before they've spoken. Babies tend to have a particular purity, innocence and sweetness about them – such as Wordsworth described so poetically when he wrote 'heaven lies about us in our infancy'.

In the best of all possible worlds, when a baby draws her first breath on entering the world, she is received into open hearts and loving and secure embraces. She blinks out at the world and, though she cannot yet focus, she basks in the loving gaze of those into whose arms she's placed. We're captivated by her purity, untainted by any convolutions of the mind. Perhaps, somewhere in our depths, we remember the glory of just being alive and ache to reclaim such honesty, trust and simplicity of expression.

In her first days a baby doesn't even know that she's in a body – she's simply inundated with new sensations and begins to process and interpret what they mean. When left unwrapped, her limbs jerk about in an uncoordinated way – she may well be surprised by the newness of this sensation. She likes being securely wrapped because until her birth she was likewise enveloped within her mother's womb. Contained within the maternal body she was at one with her mother. Nothing separated her from the source of her existence. In the first days and weeks outside of her mother's body she sleeps, feeds and blinks at the world as she begins to process a million physical impressions that are new to her.

Only 15 per cent of her brain is 'wired' for action when she arrives. This wiring involves survival reflexes which relate to hearing loud noises, being dropped, and demanding and seeking food. The other 85 per cent of her brain is waiting to be wired according to the experiences she has *after* her birth. The presence of reassuring sounds around her, the way she is lovingly held and handled, and how her needs are satisfied begin the process of laying down the remaining 85 per cent of the neural pathways in her brain – the physical part the energetic field or consciousness uses to embed itself into the body. Her brain, in turn, begins to secrete hormones, neurotransmitters and other chemicals, which flow out into her body to create an information network that affects every single one of her cells.

The baby responds instantly to bodily sensations – her pangs of hunger are a new and physical feeling for her; rumbles and grumbles, burps, farts and more all captivate her attention. As she experiences these new sensations, she sometimes expresses astonishment through vigorous crying. This in turn expands and exercises her lungs. Her brain and nervous system, full of yet-to-be-realised potential, are making trillions of connections. She lives moment by moment, having no concept of time, responding only to the immediate.

At about six or seven weeks, the baby begins to catch sight of her own body. First her hands become a source of endless fascination. They seem to have some relationship to her. In time she'll be filled with the delight of controlling their movements so that she can more fully explore her world. Impressions are laid down as she soaks up her environment, which began in the womb – where all her needs were effortlessly met – and continues now, in the outside world – where time will tell.

What is meant by 'impressions' is exactly that. Through the secretion of chemicals in response to what she feels she creates an impression in her brain – a neural pathway. Repeatedly experienced impressions create more firmly established neural pathways. Her body registers with her brain, via the nervous system, the manner in which she is held and handled. In time, the sound of the voices that calm and soothe her fill her with a feeling of reassurance. She feels with her whole being that she is loved, nurtured, cared for and wanted. The feelings evoked in her are a response to what is transmitted to her. She senses that though she's in new territory, in dramatically unfamiliar circumstances, all is well because she feels safe, valued and loved.

The feeling of being safe, valued and loved is not just a state of mind – it is also a state of physiology. Chemicals produced by the feeling of reassurance flood her body and create a platform for other experiences to follow; this process follows with all her experiences. She soaks up, like a sponge, her physical and emotional responses to the world she has entered. Her body does not just momentarily experience the feelings evoked; it lays down a chemical and electrical framework in her brain and throughout her nervous system in accordance. She lives moment by moment laying down impressions from her physical and emotional environment. These create a network for future strengthening or weakening, depending on her experiences and her reaction to them. She literally *grows* her brain and neural networks according to her experiences.

Her consciousness in the first few weeks, months and years of her life is absorbed in learning how to coordinate and operate her physical body. Her confidence in her ability to manage it grows as she becomes more dexterous and accomplishes the hurdles of supporting her own head, sitting up, rolling over, crawling, standing, walking and so on.

The other important area a baby focuses on is in establishing loving connections with those who care for her. She blossoms in an environment of love and attention. She absorbs the differing feelings engendered by her experiences as she begins to exhibit the subtle cellular language of feelings. Her smile lurches into being along with each new skill she learns – a smile made possible by the repeated patterning in her brain that leads to the secretion of 'joy', 'love' and 'happy' chemicals that in turn enable the muscles of smiling to contract.

Everyone cheers and encourages her when she attempts to sit up, roll over, take her first steps and utter a first word. Everyone beams at her, laughs and radiates love to her. It shines out of our eyes, is reflected in our smiles, is conveyed by our touch and the timbre of our voices. Even her burps and farts are a source of congratulation – sadly, this only lasts for the first year or two!

The neural impressions that the baby lays down in her brain, stimulated by her repeated experiences, might well be these: 'I am lovable, I am loved and I am loving. I am safe, valued, secure and have my place.' This is the seed of self-esteem. She knows that her needs will be met, that she is loved, wanted, valued and a source of joy to those around her. She feels a deep connectedness with those who care for her and with the world into which she has been delivered. These feelings are translated via the chemicals secreted into cellular memory. She feels her emotions with her whole body and her body becomes a living reflection of her emotional state.

By the time she has moved into her toddler years she has mastered the basics of her body. She has confidence in her ability to manipulate this vehicle she finds herself wedded to, though she has yet to master her fine motor skills and control of her bodily functions.

As she nudges two and then three years of age she comprehends that she is a separate entity from her mother. She learns about boundaries, and appropriateness with other people, animals, possessions – how to behave in the world and get along with others. This is the age when children recognise they are separate and unique individuals. Some people refer to this time as the 'terrible twos'. It's when little people realise that they can create havoc in the supermarket and that their carers can do little about it!

At this age a child is no longer an extension of her mother but an individual in her own right. By the time she's reached three she has a whole network of impressions laid down in her brain and body according to what she has repeatedly experienced.

The ability to live with confidence in one's self and one's environment and to greet each moment with an open and loving heart can be witnessed only in the very young (and not always) and in those with wisdom born of spiritual maturity.

In the baby this confidence is untested. Her heart is yet to experience the wounds of this life, her mind hasn't known fear and judgement, the world is her playground, and her body smells and feels delicious and is a source of pleasure and delight for her.

Many people mistakenly believe (or hope) that babies and young children will forget their feelings or that they're not important. Some people treat children as though they're not 'people' with all their faculties intact. But since the feelings we experience from the time of our birth stimulate the production of chemicals that literally affect every cell of the body and lay down the neural pathways in the brain for the future, our issues are in our tissues. Our personality literally becomes our biology.

Babies are fabulous absorbers of the emotional atmosphere around them – and that includes all the ambient noises that contribute to that atmosphere. For instance music and television and radio programs – and that means their content – are being experienced and interpreted, as well as conversations. Not the words and their meaning per se, but the quality of the vibration of the sound and the feelings they evoke. There is a different energy or consciousness in conversations that are angry, gossipy, bitter, resentful, frightening, negative or depressing than in loving, uplifting, wise, light-hearted and positive ones.

In time, we develop the ability to incorporate this background noise into our world and recognise it for what it is. As a child matures she becomes more proficient in the use of her senses; a young child becomes an excellent observer of whatever has captured her attention. However, a young child has a limited capacity to interpret what she is observing simply because she is drawing upon a limited history of experiences from which to arrive at an accurate conclusion.

Watch a young child studying an emotionally intense exchange. She is completely absorbed in the encounter. Have you ever seen a very young child watch a parent's face when he or she is distraught? A child is riveted by such experiences for two important reasons. Firstly, her security is being threatened because she doesn't feel safe (a necessary survival skill) and, secondly, because this is where she learns (or doesn't learn) how to deal with pain, fear, anger, sorrow, disappointment, anguish, grief or the myriad feelings she may come to know. Parents who aren't aware of, or who don't know how to live comfortably with or express, their own feelings, are unlikely to be brilliant teachers to children when it comes to giving healthy expression to *their* feelings.

For many people life neither begins nor continues as serenely or securely as described in the scenario above. Perhaps our formative years weren't spent in an unwavering atmosphere of love. Perhaps there was a confusing mixture of love and other emotions. There may have been arguments, disruption of routines, tragedies beyond our comprehension, violence, or simply a lack of attention to our needs. There may have been competition for attention from other small people who arrived before or after us. Those into whose arms we were delivered may have been immersed in their own insecurities, preoccupations, depression, busy-ness, hopes or fears, and we were little more than a distraction from, or worse, an addition to their discomfort or pain. This becomes as much a biological knowing as an experienced feeling. We begin to hear, witness and take on the subtle and not so subtle judgements of those around us.

We might gather from overheard conversations that there are people who are less or more than us. We see the values of those who care for us by the choices we see them make. In time, we inwardly dismiss that which is said but is not in fact lived by an elder. We acquire the judgements of those who care for us by reading the sub- tleties of their reactions to life. We witness their fears, cover-ups and insecurities and give them our undying loyalty, forgiveness and alle-giance nonetheless, for they are also the source of our nourishment and security.

A young child may not understand the precise meaning of words, but the feelings conveyed by body language, how her own body is treated, intonation, emphasis or hesitation in speech all speak volumes to a young mind keen to figure out how to live in the world. In this way we all accumulate a set of relatively haphaz-ard guidelines for living and conducting ourselves in the world.

In our culture, these guidelines are seldom given to us con-sciously. They're picked up through observation, experience and what we make of it or our reaction to that experience. Perhaps now, as adults, we find ourselves comfortable around love only where there continues to be confusion or pain because we know from our formative environment that love and confusion or pain are intrinsically entwined. We literally 'know' this in our cells. Through the repetitive experience of feeling a particular way we have laid down the chemical pathways that will later become 'second nature' to us. These become the basis of both our person-ality and our biology.

If a parent is unable to be emotionally available and responsive to their infant, the child may well grow up equating love with lack of emotional availability or responsiveness. In all likelihood, that young person will actively seek what is familiar to her and will 'fall in love' only with people emotionally unavailable or unresponsive to her because anything else would seem foreign.

Likewise, if a child is raised in an environment of violence, angry voices or actions then, literally, what is delivered along with the milk, whether the infant is bottle or breast-fed, is activation of the flight and fight response in the brain. What the child learns *chemi-cally* is that love, nourishment and shelter belong together with fear and activation of the flight and fight response. The two emotions of love and fear, and the chemicals thereof, are set in motion within the child, and she then seeks out relationships and situations in which she experiences what is familiar to her.

In time, our experience of the world verifies what we believe to be true about it – that it supports us in our endeavours, that it lets us down, that it can't be trusted, that it is full of opportunities or full of obstacles. As we grow older, this becomes evident in our relationships also. Whatever we believe to be true about relationships is verified by our experience and, in turn, our experience bolsters our beliefs.

By this I don't mean our daydreams about 'the perfect relationship' come true – often quite the contrary! We may hope and dream for happy relationships but if we haven't experienced them in our formative years then our cellular memory will differ from the hopes we hold. We have already laid down the neural pathways through the repetitive secretion of the chemicals we released throughout our childhood in reaction to our experiences. What feels familiar to us from our history tends to be repeated in adult life.

Hopefully, the child may have had some mitigating experiences during her growing years that have given her a truer experience of love. This might come through a grandparent, teacher, coach, mentor, friend of the family, spiritual teacher, a relative or other influence. It can happen through a chance encounter with a complete stranger.

Sometimes children become immersed in a passion from an early age. It might be studying bugs, building or dismantling things, dancing, singing, painting, the making of music, horses, sport, mathematics or a million other things. This can be for a range of reasons. It could be that a child brings with her particular gifts or interests or a quality of consciousness that will be drawn to particular interests – the body might be new but the consciousness that enlivens and permeates it is ancient and indestructible. Sometimes, if a child's life is too emotionally intense for her, she channels her energy into something over which she *does* have control and from which she derives satisfaction.

We may well forget that we are spiritual energy or consciousness foremost and believe we are just embodied personalities instead. We may lose touch with our source of power and feel bereft and hopeless. Disconnection from our source of being can lead to a life-long struggle to find meaning, satisfaction and happiness. We look for meaning and purpose outside of ourselves.

Most of us have been taught from childhood not to trust our feelings, not to express ourselves truthfully and honestly, not to recognise that we are consciousness at the very core of our being; that we're loving, powerful and creative in our true nature. Rarely do we receive support for trusting ourselves, listening to our intu-ition and expressing ourselves in a direct and clear way. We settle for what is 'second nature' to us without ever contemplating what might be our 'first nature'.

Moments of deep connection with a person – or for some children, with the object of their passion – will have significant and lifelong positive effects on a child. Through these experiences a child may have felt loved and deeply understood or caught a glimpse of a different perspective and, as they move into adulthood, will continue to seek relationships that will expand their capacity for love. Some of us emerge from our childhoods certain only of what we don't want in a relationship and uncertain of what we do want or how to go about having it.

Young babies and children are immersed in their families' con-versations and judgements. Depending on our family's beliefs, we learn to consider less, equal or more important than ourselves people from another ethnic or religious group, people who have intellectual or physical limitations, people who have less or more income, money, status, possessions or education, people with dif-ferent sexual orientations.

In some cultures, babies are immersed in a soup of fear and hatred from the time they enter the cradle: Hutu against Tutsi, Catholic against Protestant, Christian against Muslim, white against black, Israeli against Palestinian, Serb against Albanian and, of course, vice versa. It's not personal. Yet it *feels* personal. And feelings are not just states of mind; the chemicals of these feelings become embedded in our bodies through constant exposure. These judgements, based on our family's beliefs, are frequently served as an additional dish at family meals. Our judgements say that the existence of the 'other' threatens our view of the world and it always comes with the certainty that our view is right – and, in some cases, that we should be willing to kill for it, die for it.

This is how the 'sins of the father are visited upon the children, generation unto generation'. Cultural beliefs that permeate the society dictate its history. If our parents and our peers judge harshly those who are different from us then that is what we learn. From birth, we're exposed to the indoctrination of our parents' beliefs. It is here, before we can articulate a full sentence, that we learn who is 'in' and who is 'out'. We can love the people who belong to our belief system and reject those who don't fit our parents' way of seeing the world. This process occurs in every culture in society.

In our first years, we might also realise that we're not the centre of our parents' universe – perhaps we have siblings we need to share them with. The unconditional love that we (hopefully) received as an infant may now seem to have strings attached. In some families, and it seems in a great many from the stories I've listened to, children take on particular roles in order to get their needs met.

It might be that an older sibling gets a lot of positive feedback about being bright. Perhaps, in that case, the younger child may think 'bright' is not something she can achieve but that she can be fast or funny, or pretty, or quiet, or athletic, or responsible. Or she'll be the peacemaker, the 'good' girl, the black sheep; or he'll be a brave boy that never cries, or the academic one. Or any combination of these and more. We gradually cultivate, practise and accumulate a persona that will work within the dynamics of our family. We generally live out these patterns of behaviour until something stops us in our tracks and presents us with the opportunity to see things differently. Enlightenment is not about seeing different things but seeing things differently.

It is during our preschool years that we are also programmed to believe that 'I'll be happy when . . .'. 'I'll be happy when I turn five.' 'I'll be happy when I go to school.' 'I'll be happy when Christmas comes.' 'I'll be happy when I leave school.' 'I'll be happy when I find a job.' 'I'll be happy when I've found a partner.' 'I'll be happy when I have children.' 'I'll be happy when the divorce comes through.' 'I'll be happy when the children leave.' 'I'll be happy when the kitchen's renovated.' 'My life will begin again after the treatment finishes, when I move, when I lose weight, when I go on holidays . . .' always relegating our sense of contentment, peace and wellbeing to some future time when things are different from 'now'.

In this way we are trained to sacrifice the peace that's possible in the present by reminding ourselves that the future will be better. This belief also underpins some religious concepts – we suffer now but will be rewarded later.

Moment by moment we interpret our environment and respond by secreting chemicals in accordance with how we feel. The chemicals we secrete and the neural pathways they help to create gradually become both our experience of life and our biology. As our mind begins to develop we draw conclusions from this emotional and biological state. They are, after all, our experience of life thus far. In time these conclusions dictate our reactions to life and our quality of life.

All of this programming has been accomplished before we've made it to kindergarten! We've picked up our family's expectations, judgements, values, assumptions, beliefs and attitudes. We've figured out the dynamics within the family and have made significant inroads into establishing our place within it. We may not have the words to describe what it *is* that we've experienced, however, the biological consequences are eloquently expressed by every cell of our body. This unconscious biological/neural complex becomes second nature to us. It becomes our normal way to react.

As children we might have escaped into fantasy because the inner world of our imagination provided a richer or safer experience for us than the confusion of our outer physical world. We venture forth to make of our life what we will, given what we learned before and during our schooling. Through the repetition of experience the neural pathways and beliefs become more firmly established. There may well be experiences throughout childhood, adolescence and adulthood that modify, challenge, reinforce or provide different perspectives. However, we have more than the beginnings of a definition of ourselves and our relationship to others by the time we are five years old.

As we enter our school years we begin to lose the capacity to be present moment by moment, as we gather the dross of expectations, assumptions, beliefs, attitudes, hopes and judgements. We spend more time in the world of our mind thinking about 'things' – putting it all together the best way we can. We set off in good faith to seek confirmation of what we've been taught to believe.

This is the story of the prodigal son. We accompany the prodigal son on his journey believing happiness will come from external things of the world. Depending upon where our beliefs tell us this happiness will be found, we strive for qualifications, acceptance, friendships, accolades, relationships, material possessions, accomplishments, a lifestyle, perhaps power, status, money or success.

We might seek to salve inner wounds with outer distractions. We seek peace in all the wrong places, believing that the current distraction will ease the emptiness. It can become such a habit that we feel powerless to change it. Whilst pursuing this elusive happiness, we forget that we're on a journey and begin to believe the definition of ourselves we've been at pains to arrange around us. Defining ourselves by career, physical abilities or 'looks', income bracket, the house we live in, the car we drive, success or lack of it, educational status, sexual orientation, family or community standing, or whatever. All labels define us in limiting ways if they deny the existence of the spirit or consciousness that enlivens us.

The following composite story illustrates this journey away from ourselves in what Wordsworth described in the poem quoted at the beginning of this chapter as 'Shades of the prison-house begin to close upon the growing Boy'.

Donald was the long-awaited first child of an ambitious couple. His parents valued highly the lifestyle they'd achieved. Both of them had emerged from unhappy childhoods where money was short and opportunities were few and their determination to 'make it' in the world had, in part, brought them together. Their lifestyle included a luxury home on the waterfront with an indoor swimming pool, a yacht, and the holidays and social status that come with success. Their friends considered them the 'perfect couple' who 'had it all'.

Donald's parents gave a great deal of time and value to having beautiful, tanned and athletic bodies to match the impeccable outer trappings of their lifestyle. Donald's arrival was expected to complete the happy picture. However, Donald arrived with misshapen feet that would in time require corrective surgery, special boots and physiotherapy and, even then, would leave him with a limp. His mother was devastated. How could this imperfection enter their lives? There was nothing wrong physically with either her or her husband. How could Donald ski or run, let alone sail or kick a ball with his dad? Donald did not fit the dream and he was simply unacceptable. His parents related to him as if he were the *imperfection of his body* because their disappointment made it impossible to connect with his *being*.

Though Donald was raised with the toys, opportunities and education to be seen to 'have it all', what he picked up in his formative years was the distinct impression (remember, a repeated impression becomes a neural pathway) that he was a disappointment and 'less' than other people because of his physical idiosyncrasy. His self-esteem never established in a positive way, Donald set up a lifelong struggle to prove he was acceptable – especially to his parents.

Donald would often attempt physical activities beyond his capabilities to prove that he could meet the challenge. Instead of cheering him on in his efforts however, his parents would not go to watch him play sport or would turn or walk away at crucial moments. Even his best efforts proved an embarrassment to his parents and he gradually gave up trying to win their approval that way. He remembered, as a young boy, making the decision to be a material success instead. He would show them that regardless of his physical limitations, he too could be as ambitious as his parents.

In his teen years, Donald stopped doing many of the physical things he loved – sailing, golf, even water-skiing, because of the associated emotional pain of feeling he was a disappointment to his parents. He focused 100 per cent on pursuing his studies and then career, and made such a success of it that he was able to retire in his late thirties, long before his father's retirement.

However, proving himself in this way came at considerable cost. Because he *felt* deeply flawed as a human being, the financial and other successes he achieved only gave him momentary pleasure. He worked diligently to salve the inner wounds of his childhood by accumulating more and more possessions, finally well surpassing his parents in monetary wealth. But his efforts were no more than ineffectual band-aids applied to cover a wound in need of a different kind of healing.

When Donald retired, he felt depressed and quite lost. 'If I'm not what I do, then who am I?' Here he was with more than half a lifetime still stretching before him, with access to anything money could buy, and with an inner emptiness that he could no longer resist. He'd spent his life proving something to people uninterested in his efforts. He wondered about the value of his whole life since all his efforts had brought him so little inner happiness.

Donald inwardly ached for his father's respect and love but felt only anger towards him. It took courage to admit, even to himself, that he wanted anything from his father. Because when he did, he *felt* like he was the five-year-old boy all over again. He'd never wanted to feel that way again. In his teen years, Donald had decided that those emotions were too messy to deal with so he bundled up his feelings and stashed them in a corner where they quietly undermined any hope of peace.

The consequences of suppressing feelings for Donald was that he would react angrily whenever anyone ventured close to his feelings of vulnerability. Maintaining a guard to protect himself from ever feeling emotionally threatened again meant that his relationships remained quite superficial. He'd married and divorced three times and had no children – he'd decided as a young teenager that he never would, at the same time he'd decided that feelings were either too painful or hard for him to express. His mother's love was as elusive as ever and whilst she would proclaim his financial and other successes widely to her friends, Donald knew that she did so only because it cast a positive reflection on her.

Within six months of his retirement, Donald was diagnosed with cancer. The surgery and subsequent treatment proved successful. However Donald struggled to maintain his previously held façade of the successful businessman. It was as if the lid had jumped off the Pandora's box of his inner world and there was no putting the jolly thing back on again. Through the advent of cancer, Donald began to address and heal the deeper issues that had caused him so much emotional and psychological pain.

It was through one of our residential programs for people with cancer at the Quest for Life Centre that Donald saw how the patterns of behaviour accumulated in childhood had contributed to his life. These patterns had influenced his choice of partner, his career, what he valued, what suburb he lived in, how he spent his leisure time, what he read, where he holidayed, what interests he explored and with whom he socialised.

Through counselling and his own efforts, Donald continued to release himself from the patterns of the past – the shoulds, oughts, if onlys and musts of yesterday – and found a new and happier relationship with himself and a compassion for and understanding of his parents.

His fourth marriage took on a new emotional depth and the change in him brought him and his partner, June, much joy. This took some adjustment, as any change in the dynamic of a relationship brings unfamiliarity. June and Donald worked together to achieve a deeper and more compassionate understanding of one another and have a greater capacity to enjoy and share their good fortune with others.

Donald learned from his parents that other people's opinions and outward appearances were more important than he was. Like his parents, Donald had worked hard to make successful the outer appearance of his life, in the hope that it would bring him happiness through their approval and love. His and their efforts were always at the expense of inner peace and contentment.

Donald achieved that paradoxical state common to many people when diagnosed with a life-threatening illness. He was able to say that cancer was the best thing that ever happened to him because it broke him open to the potential to bring healing to the whole of his life. Put another way, it gave him an opportunity to see the second nature he had accumulated since birth more clearly and presented him with the possibility of bringing to light his first nature, which was a truer expression of himself. A confrontation with our mortality reflects the entire meaning of our life. Having seen its reflection we have the opportunity to bring changed perceptions and healing to our experience of life.

This is not only true of those who survive a life-threatening illness. People who've survived disasters, tragedies, traumas, grief and more often find a richer way of living their life from then on. It doesn't mean that we easily welcome these unexpected events yet we often find, as Joseph Campbell said,

> *It's only by going down into the abyss*
> *that we recover the treasures of life.*
> *Where you stumble*
> *there lies your treasure.*
> *The very cave you are afraid to enter*
> *turns out to be the source of*
> *what you were looking for.*

Like many other people, Donald discovered that the family into which we are born is rarely our spiritual family – that is, those people who celebrate our growth, change and blossoming. Demanding love from people incapable of giving it is a sure path to grief and misery! If the family of our blood is also our spiritual family then that is a bonus and a situation often borne out of suffering some unexpected trauma or event as a family. This kind of suffering may bring a family very close together, though there is no guarantee that it will. Maintaining expectations about what we think our family members should do, according to our view of the world, creates a great deal of anguish.

Most people who willingly embrace this deeper healing of their emotions find the hidden gifts of increased awareness and connection to their spirit, and in so doing are transformed for life.

CHAPTER 2

What Matters

Anything that is real has no beginning and no end.

Rachel Naomi Remen

Nothing that is observed is unaffected by the observer.
The nature of a thing is altered by its observer.

First law of quantum physics

What if the meaning of life was simply: we are here to learn to love.

Rachel Naomi Remen

Your life matters. You are not here by accident.
You are not a mistake. You are on the right planet.
You are not here for the kids, the career, the mortgage.
You are here to make the journey of your life via the kids, the career, the mortgage.
The journey matters more than the destination.

Me

Since recovering from leukaemia in 1984, I've worked with people like Donald facing some of life's most difficult challenges. In preparing as fully as possible for my own death I discovered a profound connection to life.

During the time of my illness I received the laying on of hands on several occasions both in Australia and in Italy. It was during these precious moments that I was transfixed by the presence of bliss; on one occasion in Italy, this experience lasted several hours and for some months after, I was able to return to this state readily.

These occurrences reminded me of an experience I'd had at the age of seven, which had also had a profound impact on me. I'd been playing with my pet dog, Brynner, in the garden when suddenly the entire physical world, including Brynner and me, became transparent and insubstantial. The earth, trees, sky, garden, house, dog and I were permeated with, and enlivened by, an indescribably beautiful light. 'Light' isn't any sort of sufficient description because this vibrating energy was full of life, indeed was life, was love, was everything. It was my essence and my source yet I had no need or ability to label it. It was an all-encompassing experience of 'being'. The only analogy I can conceive to describe it, is that it was like suddenly being the hand inside the glove – the glove being all that we relate to in the physical world.

This had been more real, more profound than anything I'd experienced until that time. I often ached for the return of its intensity. I have nudged related realms in the presence of beautiful music or in nature but this experience surpassed all others beyond measure.

This intense sense of union, of being at one with all things, nourished me in ways I didn't understand at the time. I didn't tell anyone about it as it was so beyond description. I experienced something like this 'intensity of being' or state of bliss at various times in my early life. I couldn't engineer its presence, it just happened in exquisite moments – perhaps induced by nature, music, beauty, physical pain or in moments of solitude.

Looking back, the memories that stand out in the soup of unconsciousness are those moments in which I was intensely 'present' or aware. It was because of these early experiences that I took to prayer and reading philosophical, spiritual and religious writings in my early teens. However, though they were of great interest, I never read a description that came close to capturing the rapture of that early experience. I kept it in the sacred recesses of my inner world but hindsight has revealed its presence as a golden thread throughout the fabric of my life and more prominently since the healings I mentioned earlier.

I emerged from leukaemia with a shaky hold on a remission I was assured wouldn't last. I lived in the transit lounge of life, neither here nor there, unable to commit to anything or anyone because my imminent departure was never far from my mind. However, the first few months of remission saw my health and energy increase and finally my mother asked the question my family had begun to privately contemplate – had I thought what I might 'do' now? She simply said, 'Have you thought about working, dear?'

Her words crashed into my head. Dare I contemplate living after finally accepting the inevitability of death? The return of leukaemia hovered in the background of my life: a full return to life seemed impossible when I'd been assured this remission wouldn't last. I felt like I knew how to do a 'good death' but still didn't have a clue how to live a 'good life'.

My previous training had given me the qualifications of naturopath, herbalist, homeopath, massage therapist, and yoga and meditation teacher. I'd been a vegetarian and had practised meditation since the age of 17. It had been downright embarrassing to be diagnosed with leukaemia at 32 when I was meant to know about health! All my beliefs had shattered and crumbled and left me bereft of answers.

My spontaneous reply to her shocked both of us and led me to think deeply about how I was now going to live the life that had unexpectedly been bestowed upon me. I blurted out, 'I just want to be paid for being me!'

Over the ensuing weeks I pondered what I'd meant by such a

strange remark. I knew I didn't want to live by anyone else's idea of how my life should be lived. I didn't want to play any more games of pretending everything was fine when it wasn't. I no longer wanted to say 'yes' when inside I shrieked 'no'. I never wanted to work at something just for the money. I didn't want to focus on getting it 'right' for anyone else. I'd no desire for material possessions because I knew they weren't the source of happiness. I wanted my life to mean something to *me*.

I knew a good deal about what I didn't want in my life but very little about how it could be different to the one I'd lived up until then. Many people have described this state to me when they've experienced it in their own lives; the absolute certainty about what they don't want and the uncertainty of what they *do* want.

Dolly Parton hit the nail on the head when she said, 'Find out what you love to do for work, and you'll never work a day in your life.' That's what I was seeking: a way of living that would be authentic and congruent with my values and that would be both meaningful and satisfy my needs.

There's nothing like contemplating death to sharpen our appreciation of life. I therefore found the company of others living with great uncertainty to be a deep blessing and my work with people with cancer, HIV/AIDS and other life-threatening or challenging illnesses began.

> *The remedy for dirt is soap and water.*
> *The remedy for dying is living.*
>
> Chinese Proverb

Sometimes we don't know what we think until we hear what we say. That's why creating a safe, nonjudgemental environment in which we can begin to unravel ourselves can be so helpful. That might be over a cuppa with a friend or in a group dedicated to this process or with a skilled counsellor or therapist.

Having contemplated my own death and prepared for it, only to have survived, had changed me profoundly. What gave me joy and satisfaction was seeing other people shift from feeling powerless, depressed and/or fearful to feeling that they could play an active role in what was happening to them. Through education and compassionate support the marvels of the human spirit were revealed before my eyes. These fellow travellers in the transit lounge of their own lives were wonderful companions and through the telling of their stories they helped me understand much of my own healing journey.

In my counselling and naturopathic practice, I realised the need to create a safe and compassionate environment in which my clients might meet one another and discuss their issues. Initially, these support and meditation groups took place in my lounge room at home and word spread quickly about them. Before long, more than 200 people from all over Sydney were attending the ten groups I facilitated each week. The people who came to these groups were living with cancer, HIV/AIDS, motor neurone disease and other serious or life-threatening illnesses. I facilitated other groups for their family members and for people living with grief, loss and other traumas.

My health continued to improve and for the first time in my life I felt that I was truly living the life I came here to live. I felt happy and useful even though the stories I heard were often heartbreaking. Other people soon joined me in facilitating groups and teaching meditation and our work continued to expand.

In 1990 I established the Quest for Life Foundation, a registered charity, to further this work and in 1998 the Foundation purchased the Quest for Life Centre in Bundanoon in the beautiful Southern Highlands of NSW. It is in this tranquil haven that our work continues today.

Support groups and one-on-one counselling provide a rich and powerful environment for disclosure of people's innermost thoughts and feelings. Together we developed appropriate guidelines for groups that would ensure a safe environment in which people would speak honestly and openly. These same four guidelines continue to underpin our work to this day. I believe they're also good guidelines for living in general.

The Four Guidelines

- The first is confidentiality. We don't talk about who attends a group or program or what's said there to anyone outside of that environment. Names and stories stay within the environment in which they were shared. Likewise, a person's story is allowed to find its rest and completion within those present rather than being unnecessarily repeated elsewhere.

- Secondly, we listen 100 per cent when someone is speaking. That means one person speaks at a time and we really hear what's being said rather than listening to our reaction to what they've said. For instance, if you're talking about your grief at the loss of your beloved pet cat and I'm judging that your problem is nothing compared with mine, then that's me listening to myself rather than hearing your anguish. Life's not a competition to see who's suffering the most. Each person's suffering is real and of importance to them. Likewise in life, be present to people you listen to rather than manufacturing your response in your mind while they're talking. If you're preoccupied with your response you'll miss the inflection, the hesitancy, the shift in posture or the myriad other ways we communicate beyond the use of verbal language. It is in this way that we hear what is not being said.

- The third guideline is to neither judge nor criticise. If a person feels miserable, depressed, peaceful, jealous, angry, suicidal, anxious, positive, negative or whatever, that's fine. We don't tell each other how to feel but allow enough space in our hearts to hear the feelings of another – no matter how confronting, petty or distasteful we might find them. If we think a judgemental thought, it doesn't pass our lips. In this sacred place, your truth is treasured and we're conscious you may never have spoken these words out loud before. People won't share their unspoken treasures if they feel they'll be judged for having such feelings. Likewise, judge not your self and your feeelings – let them be. They are the voice of your past experience and until awareness dawns you cannot liberate yourself from them. Judging them continues to bind you to them.

- The final guideline is to stay with our feelings rather than our theories or beliefs about things – to stay with our actual life experience rather than describing how we think things should, could or ought to be. People living up to a self-imposed standard that neither resonates with who they are or how they feel find peace elusive. We are feeling beings long before thinking ones. It is through embracing our feelings without judgement that the pathway to liberation is formed.

The atmosphere in these groups is frequently electric as people explore the deepest aspects of their existence. Illness and other significant life events can precipitate an extraordinary journey of self-discovery, acceptance and understanding – something we all crave. No wonder people often claim that having cancer or other illness is the best thing that ever happened to them! They might qualify that statement by saying they'd like the illness to go now, but they wouldn't want to lose what they've learned by having it. Being faced with death or any trauma can give us the courage to explore our depths and truly come alive. Many war veterans speak of their combat experience as the time when they felt truly alive. The presence and possibility of imminent death clarifies priorities and may provide us with unequalled opportunities for experiencing companionship, compassion and courage, and the strength, depth and wit of the human spirit.

In an atmosphere of compassion and nonjudgemental acceptance we quickly came to respect and honour one another in these groups. We drew strength and courage as we shared our hopes, fears, confusions and uncertainties. We wept buckets of tears and fell about laughing. We open-heartedly embraced each word spoken because we knew it was borne of a person's truth – and so often it resonated with our own experience of life. We became teachers and students to one another. Every moment became a precious opportunity to relinquish old definitions of ourselves, to let go of expectations of others and ourselves, to be deeply present to one another and thereby be of invaluable assistance – simply by giving the gift of ourselves to each other.

In the privacy of my consulting room we explore where peace is lacking in a person's life. I might ask, 'In what way are you not at peace?' The answers I get are as diverse as shells on the seashore.

For one person, the not being at peace might be due to some physical symptom like nausea, pain or night-sweats. For another, it might be his unhealed relationship with his father. For another, the feelings generated by an unfulfilled, unspoken dream. For some people, it's simply a case of not knowing what to eat now that they can no longer digest food in the way they used to. For others, some unhealed tragedy or long-held guilt or secret robs them of peace.

One such person was Belinda. She came to see me when she was 41 and living with advanced breast cancer with a prognosis of a few months. Part of the way through the consultation she blurted out that she wasn't sure she wanted to live. She said that she'd been living with a secret all of her life and simply couldn't continue. She wept for a while and then told me the following story.

Belinda had lived her early life with her family in the far north of Queensland. She had several brothers and their home was several kilometres from their neighbours. From the age of nine, her eldest brother had sexually abused Belinda. She loathed his visits to her room after the lights were turned off. She had tried to talk to her mother, who showed no interest. She would say to her, 'Go outside and play. I don't want to hear about it,' as soon as Belinda would start to try to tell her. Belinda made a promise to herself that she would never utter those words – I don't want to hear about it – to her own children if she had them, and that she'd always listen to their problems.

Belinda came to believe that this was what happened in most families and that it was just normal. She had confusing feelings of love for the brother who sexually assaulted her – perhaps because he gave her the odd treat to keep her from talking about it, and also because he protected her from her other brothers who likewise wanted to abuse her. She knew her place; as 'his' girl she would at least be safe from all other harm. Being 'his' girl also made her feel special, in some weird sort of way.

As a consequence of the abuse in her childhood Belinda unconsciously expected there would always be a secret price to pay for her very existence. Her feelings of shame, fear, anxiety, self-loathing and confusion remained unacknowledged and unexpressed. These experiences are stored in the unconscious and caused her to react whenever she felt vulnerable to further abuse of her as a person.

Though Belinda's feelings were unacknowledged and remained unexpressed, her body knew well what it felt like when the memory of abuse was stirred. As an adult, when Belinda had encountered situations in which she felt she was being taken advantage of or that someone expected something of her, she had often reacted out of all proportion to the actual event. This had further confused and irritated her and Belinda often heaped judgement on herself for feeling out of control. Because she suppressed the painful memories of the abuse she wasn't aware of the source of these feelings and had no language to express them. Her family had never expressed feelings clearly or directly. They had spoken more of the 'doings' of the family and did not acknowledge the feelings that its members might experience.

Growing up in a household where feelings were unacknowledged and not valued or expressed meant that the chemical consequences remained trapped within her brain and body. She *felt* great distress yet she could not easily name what it was that she was feeling. These feelings and their chemical consequences became a familiar reality for her. Belinda simply felt helpless when these feelings were present and would try to distract herself from them by keeping herself overly busy. This led to a split reality where she felt awkward and afraid in the presence of her feelings while, at the same time, she tried hard to project an image to the world that she was capable and competent.

Belinda had left home at 16 and headed for the city. She got work and looked after herself though she was often plagued by anxiety attacks and suffered with insomnia. She put these symptoms down to her move to the city and she blocked out all memories of the abuse she'd suffered right up until she'd left home. Her doctor prescribed medications for both her anxiety attacks and insomnia.

Belinda attended yoga classes in an attempt to learn to relax. But as soon as she reached a certain level of relaxation, she would be jolted back into her anxiety. She finally gave up trying to relax because she said the sensation of pressure on her chest that precipitated the jolt back into alertness was too unpleasant. It wasn't until she was telling me this story that she realised the pressure on her chest was the memory of the weight of her brother lying on top of her.

Belinda met a man who loved her and placed no sexual or emotional demands upon her. He provided stability, gentleness and kindness, and her anxiety attacks subsided though she continued with the insomnia. Belinda gave birth to a son and she was delighted. Three years later, she gave birth to a daughter and on the same day she was suddenly overwhelmed with anxiety. This anxiety was literally laid down in her cellular memory. She realised that she had recreated the same possibility of what had happened to her – the abuse by her brother, to happen between her own two children. She made a promise on the day of her daughter's birth that she would never allow her two children to be alone in a room together – and they never had been.

Can you imagine the strain of such a promise? She described one of many occasions, when she had her hands in the sink washing dishes and was suddenly seized by anxiety and had to rush to see where the children were, to make sure they were in separate rooms. This had gone on for years and Belinda had never confided in anyone about what had happened to her in her childhood. She had recreated the trade-off in her present circumstances – having to 'pay' by making herself responsible for keeping her own two children separated. Her life had no meaning without the pressure of cellular memory that told her a part of her must 'pay'.

Belinda had made her daughter into a princess who was overprotected and got her way too often for her own happiness. This lead to bitter fights between her children in which Belinda often sided with her daughter because of her need to protect her 'girl child'.

When her daughter reached the age of nine, the age at which Belinda's brother had first sexually assaulted her, Belinda developed breast cancer. Once her daughter reached puberty and started coming home from school with the dramas of teenage girls,

Belinda's anxiety attacks began again and what did she hear coming out of her mouth but the words of her mother, 'Go outside and play. I don't want to hear about it.'

We can't bear to hear in others what we're unable to deal with in ourselves. Belinda was mortified to think that she had broken her promise to herself. Her intention to never repeat what had happened to her was overridden by her body's memory of events. She was helpless to stop the reaction she felt overwhelm her. This re-action was entirely familiar to her. It is literally the re-activation of the chemical consequences of the past abuse. The feelings of fear, anxiety and confusion are not nebulous states of mind that pass into our history without consequence.

The experience of these feelings produce chemicals, neuro-peptides and hormones that affect the functioning of our bodies as they create neural pathways in the brain and body. Re-activation of this complex neural pathway becomes familiar, the needed, the constant and the expected. Belinda's 'second nature' is as chemi-cally present as it is physically enacted.

It was at this time that Belinda was diagnosed with secondary breast cancer.

Belinda wept, shook and trembled as she told this story. Finally, when the tears subsided, she looked at me dejectedly and said with a faint smile, 'I don't feel much better for having told you. I can't tell my husband because my brother's children play sport together with ours most weeks and my husband will punch my brother out if he knows what he did to me. I can't tell my mother because she'll only say, 'Why are you worried about that? It's all so long ago. You've got breast cancer – *that's* what you should be worried about!'

As it turned out, Belinda began making some very positive changes in her life. She hasn't told her husband about what hap-pened in her childhood, as far as I know, but she did tell him that she wanted to go to Africa by herself. She had always dreamed of going to a game park and decided that it was an adventure she wanted to undertake alone. Her husband was completely taken aback by this, as she'd rarely even left the state they lived in, but he was supportive nonetheless.

When Belinda's husband said he'd look after the children at Christmas so that she could go, she snapped, 'I'll bloody well go when I decide, not when it's convenient for everyone else!' And while this might seem like an unnecessarily harsh response, it was also a positive sign that for the first time, Belinda was creating her own boundaries in no uncertain terms – not skilfully, perhaps, but it was a good beginning. She duly went on her adventure to Africa – in her own time – and her health continued to improve.

I saw Belinda on and off for four years until she was quite confident in her own self-discovery and had established boundaries that were healthy and appropriate for her. Belinda had mellowed and softened around her own wounded heart and was more comfortable with her daughter's behaviours, establishing more respectful boundaries with her also. Her insomnia and anxiety had both disappeared and, at our last meeting, she was relaxed and cheerful and her health continued to support her. While she wasn't entirely free of cancer, its presence certainly wasn't impinging on her lifestyle.

Life continues to present us with opportunities to release and relinquish our 'second nature' because it is not the truth of who we are in our essence or 'first nature'. As we grow and mature in an awareness of our 'first nature', we also change our physical health. If we are dominated by what has become 'second nature' to us, then we continue the production of chemicals, hormones and neuro-peptides as a consequence of our unresolved feelings. By allowing the healthy expression of feelings and increasing our awareness of their cause, we stop *re-acting* to them and we are more able to make a more appropriate *response* to life.

For some people, lack of self-forgiveness destroys their connection to all that is sacred in the present moment. Some are seeking ways to become comfortable with their discomfort; to live peaceably in the midst of contradiction; to live their questions serenely and without an insistent expectation of answers; to keep their heart open in the caverns of hell. After all, what is the answer when a young mother with cancer looks you in the eye and asks, 'How can I have given birth to these children and now leave them?'

These questions are thrilling to me – literally – but certainly not because I have the answers. When I bear witness to the courage such questions demand, I am in awe of the spirit that enlivens us all. These are some of the sacred questions I've also contemplated. My task is not to grasp at joy or make my own or another's suffering go away, but to be with each as it comes, to witness without judgement and come to a place of compassionate understanding. In this way we come to peace by being at peace with what is. It is a privilege to be present to the deepest questions of existence.

Whilst the insights or answers stimulated by my musings are of value and relevance to me, they may or may not sustain or be of use to anyone else. However, with willingness and self-honesty we can learn a great deal from one another about how to discover our *own* best answer.

I've never focused on what to do to avoid death – certainly not when I was sick myself. I do use my knowledge of herbs, homeopathy, massage, hypnotherapy, nutrition and food-as-medicine, juices, vitamins, yoga, meditation and forgiveness practices, and so on to help alleviate people's suffering. These approaches and practices will also help someone to physically cope, as well as possible, with the medical treatments being undertaken, with a view to minimising side effects. Addressing the needs of the body in this way also helps to create an environment for healing. For me, the aim of healing is to reunite us with our spirit.

My focus is always on how to live today well. By all means drink juice, eat a fabulous diet, meditate and spend time in nature, forgive and let go the past, embrace the present fully – not so you won't die but so that you'll have lived this day well. That's the way to look back on a lifetime of days well-lived.

There are many things in life more challenging than death. Living with some unfolding nightmare in our midst can present us with an almost insurmountable challenge to our peace – perhaps a son, daughter, parent or partner living with suicidal depression, mental illness or an addiction to heroin, gambling, alcohol or risky behaviour. Loving someone with a life-threatening illness can be a living agony in itself – to be so confronted by our own helplessness or powerlessness to stop what is happening to someone we love; or being consumed by injustices from the past that have left us nothing but bitterness and resentment; living with an unbearable secret; losing everyone you love; loneliness; public crucifixion for someone else's political gain; losing your sense of meaning or identity.

These, like the advent of serious illness, are all major events or crises that cause us to stop in our tracks, review our life up until now, question the nature of who we are and how we're living our life.

Peace becomes possible when we stop blaming anything or anyone for how we feel and take responsibility for our own perceptions. If we pursue happiness in the way our culture suggests, we search for it outside of ourselves and remain dependent on circumstances that will be forever beyond our control. But if we anchor our sense of self in our consciousness, rather than in the outer trappings or events of our life, peace becomes possible. Peace is ours when we're living from the inside out, instead of from the outside in.

There is no harm in seeking happiness. Indeed, establishing peace within ourselves leads to a state of happiness. Unhappy people tend to be more self-preoccupied, socially isolated, sulky or moody and difficult to approach; happy people tend to be more resilient, forgiving, self-confident, loving, flexible, creative, humorous, spontaneous and socially at ease. Happiness is an inside job that doesn't rely on outer circumstances for its cause. Whether you live to be ten years old or 100, it's all over in a flash. Life is precious and the conscious decision to achieve peace allows us to rest on our deathbed and look back on a lifetime of meaningful memories.

It is liberating to find that there's no-one to blame for how we feel. It can be a bit disappointing as well! This realisation came to me while I was on retreat in a monastery outside Assisi in Italy during the time I was ill. Each morning I'd rise early, attend mass with the monks and then descend to the small cave in which St Francis had long ago prayed and meditated.

Initially I spent almost as many weeks weeping as meditating in that cave, as I honestly explored my life for the first time. Blaming past events for my present distress had been a pattern of behaviour for as long as I could remember. These inner wounds ached for healing, and it became clear to me that this blaming wouldn't change the fact that those things had happened to me or resolve my feelings around them.

I felt that if I allowed myself to really weep the tears within, I might shatter into a million pieces or never be able to stop crying. I had long suppressed the pain of these unhealed emotions but the combination of illness, physical weakness, self-imposed isolation and a yearning for peace finally saw my resolve to keep the floodgates shut crumble. Once these long-held emotions were allowed an outlet, my body shook, trembled and heaved as I sobbed and wailed my way into exhaustion. In bringing the light of compassion to my own painful darkness, the shadows dissolved with the tears. In weeping, the tears formed the river that lead to my heart. It is through weeping or other emotional expression that we literally release the wounded patterning of the past that is laid down in our cellular memory.

So many of us are taught, consciously or unconsciously, that to focus on ourselves and put our needs first is selfish and therefore wrong. In our culture, girls are often trained to meet the needs of others rather than their own. Boys are often taught that their value lies in the role of accomplishing things, solving problems, fixing things, making decisions. I know these are generalisations and our cultural role values are gradually changing but this thinking is deeply ingrained.

This thinking is also sick because it leads to an obvious consequence – resentment – which is one of the greatest ills of our time. Resentment isn't just a state of mind but is a batch of chemicals we secrete every time we feel that way. If we're always focused on meeting other people's needs at the expense of our own, we feel resentful. On the other hand, meeting our own needs by taking responsibility for the care of our body, mind, feelings and spiritual life is good sense. If you don't take responsibility, chances are that someone else will have to.

We yearn for healing and wholeness – for ourselves, our families, for our communities, our planet. The greatest gift you can give yourself, your family, your community and the planet is the gift of your own good physical, mental, emotional and spiritual health, by taking responsibility for how you conduct the journey of your life. We each need to find a way to live peaceably with ourselves, with the events of our lives and in harmony with our environment. Then we will find there is abundant energy left over to make a positive contribution in whatever way we feel moved to.

Many people want to know the rosy path to peace, healing or wholeness but don't want to hear about the thorny bits mixed in with the petals. People generally want the pill that will fix them rather than to take responsibility for their own perceptions and personal healing.

Waking up and being present to the challenges of life is not easy but it's immensely rewarding. Maturity demands responsibility, and that involves attaining knowledge and developing the ability to choose rather than react. Responsibility is simply our ability to respond – which is very different from an unconscious reaction.

It takes maturity to acknowledge how we feel and to accept responsibility for our perceptions. Maturity demands that we honour our experience and learn to either consciously witness our feelings or find appropriate expression for them that neither wounds others nor ourselves. If we refuse to take responsibility for our own perceptions and feelings then we maintain an expectation that life is meant to 'get it right' for us.

Letting our feelings run roughshod over other people brings no joy to us or to anyone else. At the time of an outburst, it can feel good to let out all the upset. The downside is that we often say and do things we later regret. It is possible to release the upset without wounding others and diminishing ourselves; and in the process, we reduce suffering. This conscious release also liberates us from the cellular memories stored in our tissues. Being conscious and aware of how we're living life is the first step in creating peace in our lives.

Every moment can be sacred in our life. The sacred is found when we bring the whole of our consciousness to whatever we engage in, each part of ourselves content and available for what is present in our life.

Our society promotes the illusion that life should begin with a joyful childhood and happy teen years, and that we then enter the career of our choice and excel at it, meet the perfect partner, have wonderful children who always love, honour and respect us, find our ideal home and pay it off effortlessly and all go fishing in our old age.

I'm yet to meet anyone having a life like that and it certainly hasn't been my experience!

Life is more like a roller-coaster ride. None of us knows what's over the crest or around the corner and the speed at which life travels is rarely up to us. However, it is our responsibility to find and fasten our own seatbelt; our seatbelt being the sure knowledge of how to maintain physical, mental, emotional and spiritual health and in this way anchor our sense of self within our consciousness. So when the roller-coaster unexpectedly swings to the right and we could have sworn it was meant to swing to the left, we're more easily able to accept, adjust and respond accordingly.

If we don't know what our seatbelt is or how to fasten it then we're more likely to have difficulty in dealing with the unexpected and the uninvited, let alone the unthinkable, when it happens in our life. Without the seatbelt it's easy to get stuck in, 'This isn't fair, it shouldn't have happened, it was meant to be different from this, I don't deserve this, why me?' mode. And while having such thoughts is understandable, getting stuck in that way of thinking can paralyse and embitter us. By all means rail and weep but, ultimately, to have peace we need to move beyond resisting, railing or weeping and onto acceptance.

The fact is, whatever it was *did* happen and nothing can change that. What matters is how we respond to what has happened and then moving forward in life with a sense of meaning and peace.

Once we want peace more than anything – more than wanting to be right, more than wanting to prove our worth to others, more than wanting to hold on to righteous indignation, more than wanting a cure – the whole universe will conspire to bring it about.

CHAPTER 3

Peace Matters

A life unobserved is not worth living.

Socrates

The solution to the problem of the day is the awakening of the consciousness of humanity to the divinity within.

Hazrat Inayat Khan

The longest journey you will make in your life is from your head to your heart.

Sioux saying

Inner peace is more a spiritual quality than a mental quality.
We are all here to grow in wisdom and learn to love better.
So fulfilling life's purpose may depend more on how we play than what we are dealt.

Rachel Naomi Remen

For 20 years I have been witness to the intimate stories of other people's lives. Collectively, their lives encompass every possible human drama and the full range of emotions they might evoke. Their stories have thrilled and inspired me, ripped me apart, mended me, broken my heart too many times to recall, led me into bliss, confronted, confounded and educated me, dissolved me into everything and nothing, been my heart's healing and my spirit's delight.

They have come seeking ways to enhance physical, mental, emotional and spiritual healing; to find peace and establish what is truly meaningful for them. They've come because events in their lives have caused them to stop in their tracks and ponder such profound questions as:

Who am I?
What am I doing on this planet?
Am I living the life I came here to live?
If not, why not?
And what am I going to do about it?

These are powerful questions which for some people arise in childhood or their teen years and for others are precipitated by unexpected events at any time of their lives.

Regardless of our circumstances, we can all manage the journey of life in a way that brings deep fulfilment and satisfaction. At worst, we can make the hardest times bearable and, at best, make such times fertile ground for growth in wisdom and our capacity for love and understanding.

This book does not pretend to know what is best for you or to have your answers. You have your own best answers. The words and wisdom you read here come not only from my personal experience, reflection and study but, even more so, from the tens of thousands of people who've shared their stories with me. Their lives, like your life, contain every cause of pain and sorrow as well as every cause of joy and celebration.

On finding themselves in unfamiliar territory, these people sought guidance from and conversation with others similarly challenged. Together we can explore the marvels of the human spirit.

Venturing into the abyss of our shared fears and concerns, we can shed light upon one another's path. Such sometimes agonising conversations and experiences have enriched my life beyond words.

I wrote this book with the intention of sharing how to heal your mind and emotions and change your perceptions. If you want to control or change outer events, people or the world, you might as well put this book down now.

The Questions of Suffering

So how do we live with uncertainty? What can we do to help ourselves? How can we manage fear, panic, depression, anger, anxiety, sorrow and despair? How do we heal our relationships? How do we make the right decisions? How, if we're contemplating suicide, can we find enough meaning to stay alive? How can we die and leave our children still in need of us? Is it possible to let go of the hurt in our lives? How do we find peace?

These questions are all both sacred and monumental. Sacred because they're a call to 'consciousness' or 'being'; a call that requires more of us than we've been using up until now. Monumental because they provide the opportunity to shift our awareness profoundly and dramatically.

These ancient questions, uttered throughout history by all those who suffer or contemplate their meaning, bring us to attention and provide us with an opportunity to explore the nature of who we are.

We all crave a life free of suffering, but look around. Whether the suffering is physical, emotional, mental or spiritual, suffering is universal. If you didn't want suffering, wrong planet! How do we live skilfully in the midst of suffering – how can we keep our hearts open, compassionate and loving? How can we make a practical and valuable contribution towards easing the presence of suffering in others and ourselves?

Suffering, in a deeper context, is how we feel when we're not in balance – when we're not at peace, when we're living from the outside in. In this way, we all suffer from time to time – when we're not at peace with the events of our lives; when we fear the future; if our relationships aren't fulfilling; if we're always pressured by time; when we feel overwhelmed by life; when we feel disconnected from ourselves.

It is in the midst of upsetting events in life – the diagnosis of illness, the death of a loved one, an unexpected loss or disappointment – that unsettling questions about ourselves might surface. We're often caught unawares by these questions and can be perplexed about why, in the face of the current trauma, we're also having to face unresolved issues or questions from the past.

Because of world events – escalating terrorism and global unrest, the pressures of overpopulation and declining natural resources, the mounting distress of refugees seeking a safe haven for their families, the threat and manifestation of war – questions about the meaning and purpose of our lives have surfaced for many people. Suffering is no longer something that we associate with distant parts of the world. It's here on our doorsteps, indeed, it's in our lounge rooms.

Likewise, our values are constantly being reviewed and re-appraised as we contemplate issues related to cloning, the genetic engineering of our food supply, terrorism, religious differences, the manipulation and distortion of facts, corporate collapse through unethical behaviour and a host of other daily offerings from the media. Many people are reviewing how and with whom they spend their time. Interest in leisure activities is increasing. People are reconnecting and spending more time with family members, friends and loved ones.

Some people have glimpsed and pondered the big questions about their own existence, then allowed them to recede into the background of their lives. Often, if there are no easy answers or disappointment with what they find, people will bury themselves in their area of competence – mothering, working, sport – at the expense of creating a healthier balance in their life. Other people feel the presence of these questions as an unsettling undercurrent throughout their life. But regardless of how these questions might arise, the urgency with which they're uttered increases dramatically when we're in crisis.

Why are so many people everywhere now asking these same questions? Because, increasingly, we are sensing that our personal lives and the societies we live in are not on a path that leads to balance and peace. Increasing numbers of people are looking for deeper fulfilment in their spiritual, mental and emotional lives. We are searching for greater meaning and purpose, and for ways to live more responsibly and harmoniously with each other and our planet.

The world as we know it is constructed without respect for the emotional and the spiritual or an understanding of the fundamental consciousness that underpins human life. It is a representation of our desire to dominate nature rather than to live in harmony with her and this desire has overridden commonsense to the point that it is now a rarity.

We've lost faith in our own ability to discern what is good and true for us. Indeed, we're now encouraged to have no faith in commonsense until it is scientifically proven. And one of the major flaws in the scientific model that dominates is that it relegates a person's individual experience to the anecdotal. Science is content with the average without studying the exceptional. It speaks only of 'groups of people' and lacks interest in the individual's experience. Of ourselves we know nothing and must rely on experts to inform us. We then rely on outer interventions to treat what is often borne of inner causes.

The Western world values the mind and its rationalism highly. In addition to sport, the scientific tradition of having to prove everything has become our religion. We are taught that reason, logic and consistency are paramount – indeed they are the highest truth. This model encourages us to suppress our emotions and relegates feelings, intuition, faith or irrational behaviour to the less consequential at best and considers it a nuisance and a sign of weakness at worst.

We may feel a disquieting sense of anxiety about our life or find our fears of the world increasing. We have lost faith in the structures of our society because we feel the people who enliven them are likewise lost – our decision-makers, our political representatives, our law-makers, our educators, our medical providers and our church leaders. We've lost faith in many of our institutions themselves as well as the people in positions of leadership within them. The challenges that face us in establishing what we all say we want – peace – can seem overwhelming.

Distraught we may well be when we helplessly watch so many young people and others take their lives. We may feel that the destruction of the environment is spinning out of control. We may be privately grieving for the forests and their creatures and plants that are rapidly becoming extinct. Many quietly grieve for the inequities against indigenous people everywhere who have so long been ravaged by our greed and the wanton destruction of their habitat and lifestyle. We may feel apprehensive about the Pandora's box that biotechnology and genetic engineering have already opened. We may feel deeply disquieted by witnessing ourselves, and society as a whole, valuing things that we know won't draw us closer to peace.

The rate of change in some aspects of life and some areas of the world is so rapid now that what was taken for granted yesterday may be obsolete tomorrow; in others, it still grinds all too slowly. That is not to say that there aren't many positive changes taking place in our own awareness and in our communities, and it is precisely this shift in consciousness we all crave. We want a more meaningful expression of ourselves, a more spiritually aware and fulsome way of living based on a richer and more compassionate perspective.

As a society, we've focused on the development of the physical and mental aspects of life at the expense of the emotional and spiritual. Our lives are out of balance and we're struggling to find equilibrium in the midst of rapid change.

If we're to make a positive contribution within our community and manage the journey of our own lives effectively, we need two essentials – well, perhaps three. Firstly, we need to develop our resilience and flexibility. Secondly, we need to be grounded in an inner stability that is unwavering, which leads us to a life based in a conscious awareness, lived from the inside out. And, thirdly, it's simply not worth coming to the planet unless you cultivate a persistent sense of humour.

Only through letting go our need for control of outer circumstances, and with it our judgement about how things should or should not be, will we find the inner stability to see us through these change-filled times. This inner stability can be the foundation of our lives. From this place of clarity and peace we can make a more meaningful and appropriate response to life's challenges.

There are many things in life that we cannot change; the weather, a diagnosis, a loss, an accident, an injury, a disappointment. The question that confronts us is: Who do I want to be in relation to this? Do I want to feel a helpless victim of my circumstances or do I want to actively participate in meeting this challenge? Will I surrender my power in defeat or look the monster in the eye? Can I see it as an opportunity or only as a threat? Will I allow it to embitter and affect me henceforth or will I use it as a gateway to deeper realisation, compassion and wisdom? Will I let it define me or am I more than that?

I mentioned the weather as a simple illustration of something we cannot change. On waking to a soggy wet morning, some people grumble, leave bed then home reluctantly and stay grumpy all day. Meanwhile, a neighbour wakens to the same soggy morning, leaps out of bed in delight, pulls on wet-weather gear and takes a long, enjoyable walk in the rain. The rain just rains. Some people get wet;

some people walk in the rain. How we think about the rain is up to us. How we feel about wet days is dictated by our beliefs. For one it's a misery, for another a joy. Neither is right. One has more fun.

If I believe that wet days are devoid of fun then I'm bound to have a miserable time if I visit India in the monsoon season. Allowing outside circumstances to dictate my reality is fraught with uncertainty, pain, confusion and disappointment.

We each grew up with a whole range of beliefs about ourselves, about life, relationships and more. They were taken on unconsciously as part of the fabric of our family. Many of our beliefs, which are based on reactions to life experiences, have been accumulating since childhood.

When we hear ourselves say, 'That's just how I am,' or 'That's just who I am,' or 'That's just how I do things,' beware! Ancient patterns are at work and we're admitting that we have no control over them. It can be a very convenient way of staying stuck! For instance, many people use bluster and a loud voice to intimidate others rather than acknowledge a more honest acceptance of their vulnerable feelings. Repelling people who come close to our emotional wounds may seem easier than trying to heal them. However, we cause ourselves much suffering by maintaining behaviours that undermine any hope of peace.

The problem is that we're often not aware of having these beliefs or of how they colour our lives in ways that deny us peace. We look at the world through the coloured lenses of our accumulated beliefs. Each belief adds depth and more colour to the lenses we wear. It's the way we see things. It's what we believe to be true. It is second nature to us to see things that way.

And that is precisely the point – these lenses do not reflect our first nature, our essential consciousness; they can only reflect back to us a view of the world supported and distorted by our accumulated beliefs. We'll also search out others who enjoy wearing the same coloured lenses as ours, which assures us our beliefs are right.

But it might be time to question some of the lenses we hold up to the world and see if they still serve us well.

The choice to see things differently provides us with a tremendous point of power. With this change in outlook we can choose our response to life rather than just react according to our habitual beliefs about others and ourselves. And this act of choice is a key to establishing peace in our lives and to living a spiritually based life. Choice is a present-time activity and peace is found in the present.

Understanding Spirituality

The spiritual is considered inconsequential by people who need it to be scientifically validated. That is changing, indeed has changed, as quantum physics acknowledges the interconnectedness of all things and the purpose served by the creation of the universe. As we understand more deeply the energy or consciousness that permeates, enlivens and *is* the universe, we will more deeply value the possibilities that living in the present moment bring.

We create as sacred each moment that we bring the whole of ourselves to. A spiritually based life is one in which we consciously manage our physical, mental and emotional aspects: a life in which interconnectedness and wholeness is experienced, honoured and cherished.

Each moment of our life is an opportunity to be present to its unfolding. So often our minds, filled with their incessant chatter, rob us of the precious opportunity to be present to life's wonder and possibilities.

From listening to many stories and reflecting on my own, it seems that we all want the same thing: peace in our lives. Peace within ourselves, within our families. Peace in our communities, throughout our nation, on our planet.

Don, in his mid-30s, was in his last weeks of life when I visited him at home. He'd been a devoted schoolteacher and a lover of the theatre and opera. For many months he'd been a volunteer at the Quest for Life Centre, answering the phone and counselling others who were living with a life-threatening illness or were struggling with some other significant challenge.

On this particular day, when he could no longer leave his home, Don and I sat hand in hand in his lounge room opposite an open window. With an air of profound peace and contentment he said, 'Sometimes when I sit here, the smell of freshly brewed coffee wafts in through the window from the café downstairs. Sometimes I hear snatches of conversation from the pavement below. Occasionally two little sparrows sit on the garage roof outside and sing to one another. I can't imagine heaven can be any nicer than where I am right now.'

Don could have as easily been consumed with rage and despair at the limitations and suffering his disease placed upon him or with resentment and bitterness that his young life was now at an end. He chose differently.

Heaven lies within us and is available to us all. It is not a geographical destination that we enter at some future time. Hell is that state in which we feel separate from everyone and everything – abandoned, lost, forgotten by life or love. It is a moment-by-moment choice whether we live in heaven or hell. Our life's purpose is to awaken to heaven because it's here, now. Practising peace is the gateway to heaven.

Peace, however, is no passive, wishy-washy state of acceptance. Peace is a dynamic state in which we feel fully alive and able to embrace each moment with an open heart and a clear mind, regardless of its challenges. It embodies living from the inside out, anchoring our sense of self in the realm of consciousness rather than in the outer physical circumstances of our life.

The following four qualities provide a practical framework to understand what peace of mind is and how it can be a living presence in our lives. These four qualities underpin my work, my life and this book. You will see the practical application and consequence of living with them intertwined throughout these pages. It can be useful from time to time to revisit these qualities until you feel quite familiar with their essence. They are as applicable to the individual as to our nation and the wider global community.

The presence of these four qualities is always found in people who have spontaneous remissions or who far outlive their doctors' predictions. However, although these qualities might impel these individuals to *do* all kinds of things and, when and if they attain a remission or cure, they might write or talk about what they *did* to make themselves well, they are completely missing the point. It is the qualities *themselves* that are of value rather than what the qualities might inspire an individual to *do*.

For instance, someone with these qualities might read about macrobiotics and become completely inspired by the philosophy and concept because it feels right for them. They go all out for macrobiotics, achieve a cure and then write a book called *Macrobiotics Cured My Cancer*. It may appear that the value lies in our 'doing' when in reality it lies in the quality of our 'being'.

I know people who are alive and well today who were given months, weeks or, in a couple of cases, hours to live, many years ago. None of their so-called terminal diseases were the same and they might have approached their situations very differently but what they each had in common were these four fundamental qualities.

These qualities are not just a state of mind but a state of physiology – one that is positively conducive to physical healing and creating wellness. These qualities also exist in people who choose to liberate themselves from the limitations that life, their upbringing or other people might place upon them.

As each quality begins with the letter 'c' they're known as the Four Cs[1]:

---

[1] These four qualities underpin our work at the Quest for Life Centre in Bundanoon and have been supported by research into spontaneous remissions by Caryle Hirshberg and Brendan O'Regan of the Institute of Noetic Sciences.

1. The first necessary quality is that we have a sense of **control**
   over our responses to life; we consciously choose our
   response to life's challenges rather than react habitually
   from the past. It requires us to be present to life's challenges
   rather than staying stuck in repeating what has gone before.
   This enables us to continue growing in wisdom and
   understanding, and recognises that life is not static and that
   there is no one 'right' approach to it. This quality allows
   diversity and spontaneity and a willingness to learn from
   wisdom borne of history. By listening to the voice of our
   consciousness – our intuition – we become active
   participators rather than helpless victims – we recognise that
   while we can't always change what happens to us, we can
   change our response to what happens. This enables us to
   celebrate, honour and respect our individual path. It's fine
   to go through the 'Why me? It's not fair!' stage, but we
   don't want to get stuck there. We need to move on and say,
   'This *did* happen; now what am I going to do about the fact
   that it did?'

2. The secondly quality is to feel **committed** to living – to be
   willing to get emotionally up-to-date with our life. This
   quality is often the most challenging of the four as it
   requires us to take complete responsibility for our
   perceptions and to stop blaming or resisting what is. This
   quality may involve a refocusing of priorities, dealing with
   issues of forgiveness – of both others and ourselves – or
   resolving relationship or communication difficulties. To live
   wholeheartedly in the present we need to resolve the issues
   of the past. We may need to weep about what happened to
   us, rail at it, write about it, talk about it, paint it, sing it or
   scream it until we arrive at that place where we can say,
   'Yes, that happened to me. I've gleaned the wisdom from

the experience but I'm no longer living with the woundedness of it'.

Our priorities may have been skewed by the 'I'll be happy when . . .' story that motivates many people; we're forever postponing our sense of happiness and peace to some future time when our life will look different from how it is now. A deep commitment to our life understands that happiness is an inside job rather than an inner state derived from an outer circumstance; it recognises that peace is always possible now, not in five minutes time, nor five minutes' past.

With this quality we ask ourselves and deal with questions like, 'Am I going to allow the events of my history to dictate my reality, or can I be more than that?' and 'Do I want to use as an excuse what happened in my past to justify my actions in the present?' With this quality we realise that the happiest relationships are built on a foundation of forgiveness – of others, of life circumstances and of ourselves.

It sometimes takes great courage to be honest with ourselves and our loved ones, and to communicate about our inner fears and vulnerabilities. This is particularly so if a relationship has deteriorated into a superficial or habitual reaction to someone. Improving communication within relationships takes willingness, honesty and effort. Our primary relationships require constant awareness and work to keep them current, fresh and full of spontaneity, humour and life.

3. The third quality is that we feel **challenged** and excited by life. What is it that gets our juices flowing and our eyes sparkling? Are we living our lives with a passion for who we are and what we do? Are we living the life we came here

to live? Are we spending our time in a way that feels meaningful for us? Can we find meaning in our suffering?

A pearl only comes about because something irritated the heck out of an oyster. In the same way, suffering can become a path to liberation because it pushes us into exploring parts of ourselves that we'd never have ventured into otherwise. It is suffering that breaks us open to compassion, wisdom and understanding. If we're unwilling to bring the light of our consciousness to the exploration of our vulnerabilities, we remain trapped in their darkness. With a sense of adventure and challenge in our hearts we might perceive instead that every event has the potential to transform us, and that disasters are particularly valuable in challenging and changing our thinking.

With this quality of challenge comes the precious meaning of each moment in life. It gives us the opportunity to listen to the voice of our spirit and respect its wisdom. It leads us to honour and respect ourselves and the journey of our life with the understanding that nothing bad or wrong is happening to us. If we act as if every event has a purpose, then our whole life will have a purpose.

This quality embodies faith in the notion that all is unfolding in its own perfect way and in its own perfect timing. It also requires that we do not take our lives so personally; to understand that life does not have a vendetta against us.

4. The final quality is a sense of **connectedness** – feeling that we're loved and supported by those with whom we share our life and having a sense of belonging or place; or feeling that we're connected to what we consider sacred within ourselves and our environment. This sense of belonging might be to our intimates within family and close friends

or it might be to a group, community or the global family
of humankind. Its essence is about an appropriate valuing of
self both personally and in relation to life and other people.

With an understanding of the value of these four
qualities in establishing peace within ourselves, we begin to
see the events of our life differently.

Commonsense tells us that anyone who feels completely out of
control of their life, is ambivalent about living, feels that all their
challenges are overwhelming and that no-one loves them or that
they don't belong anywhere, won't fare nearly as well as someone
for whom the opposite is true.

Inner peace can then be described as a feeling in which we're
content, resourceful and capable; in which we're present to witness
and participate in each moment; in which we're passionate and
open to life; and in which we love and value ourselves and our relationships with others.

The study of the effects of emotional states on the body has
revealed that peace of mind is not just a state of mind but is also a
state of physiology. Moment by moment our brain and other parts
of our body secrete chemicals in accordance with what we are
feeling. We know what anger feels like – it's not just a state of mind
but a state of physiology. We know what fear feels like – we don't
just experience it in our mind, we feel its presence in our body.

Throughout life we're confronted by challenges to the full and
positive presence of the qualities of peace. Our experience of these
four fundamental aspects of peace dictates our quality of life. In this
way, we significantly contribute, either positively or negatively, to
our physical health. The feelings engendered by the presence or
absence of these qualities contribute moment by moment to our
health through the chemicals we secrete. And thus we can manage
the journey of our lives most effectively by taking responsibility
for the positive presence of these four qualities within ourselves.

Who might manage this journey, then? It is the wise, humorous, loving, powerful, compassionate, creative spirit that we are in our essence. If we're disconnected from the wellspring of our consciousness, we might well feel lost, empty, fearful, depressed or a deeply personal kind of meaninglessness.

The concept of our true essence or consciousness being spiritual is not a religious one. Our religious beliefs may be our chosen path by which we access and explore our consciousness, but such beliefs are not necessary to the development of consciousness or the experience of it in daily life.

Indeed, many religious beliefs may well be opposed to the individual's experience and judgemental of it. In most instances, people born into religions are raised according to the customs and practices upheld by that tradition. These customs and expectations are not felt intuitively by the person but must be learned and obeyed. They form an orthodox structure outside of a person and are not dependent on the individual's perception or experience. In this way religious practices can provide a useful means by which we give our spirituality expression. However, they can become stifling or ineffectual if they limit an individual's experience of their own essential nature.

Any teaching that doesn't allow lessons to be learned through individual experience is not a spiritual teaching but is a form of indoctrination. Life lessons become true for us when they're learned through a balanced and open communication between our heart and mind. Teachings have nothing to do with rigid concepts and moral absolutes. We can choose to see our lives as an opportunity for growth and learning, to allow our mental and emotional experiences to become opportunities through which we learn to resent or respect, discard or accept, to control or liberate.

Sometimes we don't discover that we're not living the life we came here to live until the uninvited, the unexpected or the unthinkable happens. We generally learn the greatest lessons at the time when the going gets rough. It's often when disaster strikes, when we get knocked back or when our worst nightmare happens that we wake up and say, 'Something's got to change, and it's me.' Events such as the diagnosis of serious illness, being retrenched, an accident, the death of a loved one, an alarming world event, getting sacked, rejected or abandoned, retirement or any trauma or tragedy can cause us to reflect upon our life until now, question its value and purpose, and seek a more meaningful way forward.

However, people ponder these same questions without the occurrence of a major or minor calamity. We might as easily stumble into such questions when our heart is unexpectedly pierced by beauty or love; when we turn 20, 30, 40 or more; if we're overtaken by wonder at nature; when we're transformed by a piece of music; when we look into the eyes of a child, a dolphin or a whale; when we find that we're pregnant and become more thoughtful about bringing new life onto the planet. Sometimes we simply become aware of a yearning for something that's missing.

To focus on our physical and mental abilities at the expense of our more subtle depths is to deny the whole of who we are. The balance that comes about through the healthy integration of all aspects of ourselves leads to choices that are sustainable, just and compassionate, both in our personal lives and in our wider community.

Most of us were given little guidance in how to skilfully manage our own life, let alone anyone else's. And so, especially given the nature of the changing times in which we find ourselves, how are those of us charged with being parents or carers of children meant to pass on that which we haven't experienced or don't ourselves really comprehend? It is no-one's fault that we find ourselves in this predicament – unsure of how to live our life so that it brings us deep satisfaction and fulfilment, and even less sure of how to support and educate our young people in managing their life's challenges, which are often new and different from those we faced.

Your life matters. You are not here by mistake, by chance. You are here to make a contribution that can only be made by you. Your value does not lie in what you do but who you are. *You* are the gift. We are here to release all that is false or limiting about ourselves and to grow and blossom into all that we truly are.

The people I've journeyed with have been on an accelerated path to realisation precipitated by illness, grief, loss of meaning, trauma, depression, anxiety or tragedy. Their need for peace was urgent and all-consuming. The discoveries and insights they and I gleaned together will, I hope, speed your own journey to self-understanding and give you valuable tools to transform your life in a way that is meaningful for you.

If what you read resonates with your own commonsense and reason then, by all means, make good use of it and see if it's of value to you. If anything you read doesn't resonate with your own commonsense and reason, then let it go – no-one knows you better than you do. You are the world authority on you. Don't give the power of your own discernment and discrimination away to anyone.

You are not your body; you have a body. It is your responsibility to nourish it, rest it, exercise it and 'fluff it up'. You are not your mind; you have a mind. It is your responsibility to bring it to rest so that you can hear the voice of your intuition, your consciousness, and to keep your mind in good company. You are not your emotions; you have emotions. It is your responsibility to learn how to witness your feelings or express them in ways that neither wound yourself or others. You are consciousness, soul, spirit, energy, life. Anchoring your sense of self in your consciousness is the path to living from the inside out.

One way in which you can consciously embrace this path is by focusing on the physical care of your body. It is in your physical body that you glimpse the deeper reflection of your mental and emotional aspects, and through caring for it you care for the temple that houses your consciousness.

CHAPTER 4

Physical Matters

You are not your body. You are more than your body.

Health is not the absence of disease.
It is a dynamic state of being in which we feel fully
alive and able to embrace the present moment with
an open heart and a clear mind.

Me

Our attitude toward nature and our own bodies has
been one of conquering and controlling rather than
respecting, honouring and cooperating.

Shakti Gawain

Science too often ignores the spiritual dimension of
life, while the mechanistic model of medicine treats
the body as a machine without a heart.

Gail Bernice Holland

Our body is our spacesuit for planet Earth. We cannot come here and have a human experience without a body. Of course, the analogy of the spacesuit is only that – an analogy. Our body is intrinsically wedded to and affected by our mind, emotions and spirit. However, there's value in seeing ourselves as embodied rather than our physical bodies being the identifying feature of who we are.

Our body is an awe-inspiring, self-healing, living expression of our consciousness. We contribute moment by moment to our health by the quality of our awareness and the secretion of chemicals, pheromones, hormones, neuropeptides and neurotransmitters in response to our feelings. Any imbalance or blockage in our spiritual, emotional or mental aspects will eventually be translated via these chemicals into our physical body.

In addition to our genetic predispositions, what we put into and onto our body will determine its health. Are you a friend to your body, cooperating with its own marvellous potential to self-heal? Do you treat your body as if it were the temple in which you reside? Do you replenish it with fresh, simple, whole foods? Do you give it pure, uncontaminated water? Do you fill your lungs with fresh, clean air? Do you exercise it regularly and 'fluff it up' to make it feel good? Do you rest and refresh it through deep relaxation and adequate sleep?

People often spend a great deal of money and endless hours focused on improving the way their body looks at the expense of caring for the being that enlivens it. People might believe they've got it together by making their physical body look good or function well. It's easy enough to fall into the trap of believing that we *are* our bodies when so much emphasis is placed upon that premise in our society.

Attaching our sense of self to our physical body can be tricky, though. What if we lose our looks or fitness, become sick, disfigured or disabled? What about when we grow old? Our world shrinks rapidly if we use our physical body as our main source of identification. It's part of living from the outside in instead of the inside out.

Many people use their body as a marker for how they're doing on other levels. For instance, if we focus on improving our physical health with an attitude of having to earn our recovery from an illness, then we may be disappointed if our body doesn't seem to respond in the way we believe it should. I often say to people with life-threatening illnesses, 'Don't drink juice, take vitamins and supplements, improve your nutrition, forgive everyone and meditate so you won't die. By all means, drink juice, take vitamins and supplements, improve your nutrition, forgive everyone and meditate so that you *live today well*.' In this way we can set about overwhelming ourselves with wellness. The outer action might be the same but the intention and motivation are completely different. Don't focus on preventing death but on increasing life. Intention is everything.

Having people relate to you as if you are only your physical body can leave the inner being hungry for attention. It is for this reason that I generally prefer to say to people living with grief or the challenge of illness, 'Do you feel as good as you look?' This gives people permission to say, 'No! I feel rotten and I'm sick of everyone telling me how fabulous I look!' To say, 'You look fabulous!' can sometimes mean, 'I've decided that you're okay, because you look okay. I don't want to hear how you feel because I might not know what to say and I don't want to feel uncomfortable.'

This applies equally to all of us. If we value ourselves only by how our body looks to others or its physical accomplishments, we're destined for disappointment if and when our body changes.

Indeed, we might continue this identification with the physical, believing that once we have the right environment around us – the right clothes, partner, children, house, jewellery, car, bank balance, holidays, accolades, job, friends, associates, and so on – we'll be happy.

What happens, though, when through illness or other unforeseen event we lose everything – the job, house, car, partner, money, accolades, friends, associates all gone because of the unexpected or because we're unable to maintain them. If we believe that success is measured by a collection of accoutrements, then we're bound to have a crisis of identity when they're stripped from us.

The emphasis on making our life look good to others dominates many people in our culture. If only we can get our body looking fabulous and our life looking successful, then we'll be happy. Some people wear their house or car as a badge of accomplishment. Imagine attaching your sense of self to the car you drive, only to feel mortified when it gets scratched!

There's nothing intrinsically wrong with having all our physical needs met and being surrounded by beauty and the comforts of our choice. Indeed, it's a natural consequence of managing life well that we derive an adequate income to support ourselves and which enables us to physically thrive in the world. The problem arises when we believe our value is *dependent* on those physical attachments – including our body.

To find that peace is possible regardless of what's going on in our body or physical world is a blessing. Experiencing a deep sense of equanimity and security within ourselves when change and disintegration surround us is an accomplishment we're all capable of. All of us who've had the physical challenges of serious illness, disability or disfigurement have been faced with the need to reappraise who we are. If we're to have peace, we need our sense of self to be anchored in our being, not in our body.

The realisation of impermanence is paradoxically the only thing that we can depend on. The only law in the universe that never changes: that all things change and that all material things are impermanent.

When I had leukaemia, my mind and body shrieked a million things at me. My life as I knew it was ending. My young children would be left without a mother; my parents would grieve another child – my middle brother having died through suicide not long before my illness; my eldest brother would mourn another sibling. What had my life amounted to and how could I inflict further pain on those who loved me by dying? The powerlessness and helplessness I felt were an agony. It felt like sinking into quicksand.

In time, through the practice of meditation, my preference became to live on as 'Petrea' – but I wasn't addicted to having to stay in a body in order to have peace. If I could only have peace if I stayed in my body, then death would always be fearful for me. I embraced the feelings around my death in order to lose my fear of them.

Peace is always possible because it's a moment by moment choice. And peace is not just a state of mind; it is a state of physiology – one that is positively conducive to creating real health.

We're emerging from a time when we believed health to be haphazard, as much dictated by good luck as anything else, and that we had little to do with its creation. When things went wrong we trotted off to the doctor who prescribed some magic for our ailment.

Over the last 20 years or so, we've begun to take more responsibility for the creation of our own health. Through education we know about reducing dietary fat, increasing exercise, eliminating smoking and the excessive drinking of alcohol, and reducing overly refined foods, hydrogenated oils and coffee. Many people have increased exercise, dietary roughage, vegetables and fruits because of this education.

When I began working with people with cancer 20 years ago, cancer councils and oncologists (cancer specialists) proclaimed that diet had nothing to do with the formation of cancer. Now it is widely accepted by those same groups that at least 35 per cent of cancers are diet-related and far more are created through lifestyle factors.

The briefest visit to the zoo shows that veterinarians are passionate about feeding the animals in their care appropriately. There are signs requesting us not to share our food with them because an unnatural diet will make them sick. Their attention to the dietary needs of sick animals is even more stringent.

Doctors caring for our athletes are very particular about their diet – the athletes', not necessarily their own! So are racehorse owners. So why would we trivialise diet for people who are sick? It seems an amazing arrogance to believe that we're somehow different from other physical creatures and, indeed, are superior to them – that we can ingest whatever we like without consequence. It is testament to the extraordinary capacity of our bodies that they process, eliminate or find ways to cope with what many people think of as foods – substances that were never designed to be digested by the human body.

For 60,000 years plus, human beings have eaten organic produce off the land or out of the sea. We dried our food or used salt to preserve it. Since World War II we've been doing things with our food supply that have never been done before in the history of humankind. We've added more than 100,000 new chemicals – not previously in existence in the universe – to our environment. (We develop about 9000 new chemicals each year, which we likewise introduce into our environment, and 90 per cent of all of these chemicals are carcinogenic.)

There's not a human being on the planet now who doesn't have traces of dozens of these chemicals in their body. That means there's not a woman on the planet who can provide a toxic-free pregnancy or toxic-free breast milk.

Some years ago medical researchers seeking to establish the effect of chemicals on our bodies looked for a population to use as a control group. They tested the indigenous Inuit people from Alaska in the expectation that they'd be unaffected by pollutants as they adhered to a traditional diet. However, because these people are at the top of the food chain, they had ingested high levels of persistent toxic chemicals. These chemicals find their way to the bottom of the sea where they are ingested by microscopic creatures; these are then ingested by the next size of creature up the food chain until they reach the fish, then the seals, then the polar bears and then the Inuit. Our bodies were never designed to process these chemicals that don't belong in our environment and some of which mimic the hormones human bodies produce.

We now add chemical preservatives, flavourings, colourings, emulsifiers and sweeteners to our food. Some of these chemicals are already implicated in neurodegenerative diseases of the brain. We don't replenish our soils with organic compost but with chemical fertilisers. We spray poisons on produce while it's growing, pick it before it's ripe, store it too long, transport it too far, then gas, freeze, can or package it. We seem easily taken in by the look of a food without any enquiry about where, when or how it was grown. We've been seduced by convenience, jingles and packaging.

Many people no longer value the joy and satisfaction of purchasing fresh food and preparing healthy and nutritious meals. Convenience and the pressures of time mean that many city apartment kitchens are now designed without a stove or traditional oven. The only appliances are of the plug-in variety including a microwave and small refrigerator.

The full outcome of tinkering with the genetic constitution of plants and animals can only be guessed at. What is the motivation of those attempting to dominate, mould and control creation by manipulating genes according to the wishes of those who will finance this manipulation? The argument for continuing to modify plants and animals genetically is based primarily on economics – and a good argument can be made, but only if economics is more important than people. Remember that not so long ago it was considered appropriate practice to incorporate animal tissue in the feed of animals that normally ate none. What does your commonsense say about the idea of feeding cows ground-up bones and offal? That too was a decision based on economics. Likewise the introduction into the Canadian environment of genetically modified canola has led to it being the 13th most common weed in that country.

When they develop cancer or another illness, some people choose to eat organically grown produce. However, we could all be agitating for organically grown produce now – not waiting until cancer or some other degenerative disease takes hold. Much of our urban lifestyle removes us from the cycles of nature and we don't have a relationship with the production of our own food supply. Growing even the smallest amount of our own food brings great satisfaction and joy. Anyone who's ever eaten freshly picked fruit and vegetables straight from the garden will attest to the sense of fulfilment it brings, as well as the fabulous flavour and excellent nutritional value.

We need to think about what we're doing now and not wait until it's been scientifically proven to be detrimental to our health. Learn to listen to your own body and rely on your intuition, reason and commonsense in choosing appropriate ways to nourish and replenish your body. Below are several nutritional facts and issues for you to consider.

- In Australia in the years between 1900 and 2000 the average person's yearly consumption of sugar rose from half a kilogram to 75 kilograms. There simply haven't been enough generations in that time to make the physical evolutionary adjustments necessary to accommodate such a dramatic increase in just one substance that isn't even a food. Our diabetes rates are soaring in both children and adults yet there hasn't been a single scientific report that highlights the massive increase in sugar intake. Sugar is an addictive substance that our body craves. It occurs naturally and in balance with nutrients when we ingest it in fruits and vegetables.

- For many Australians, the average transit time from when they eat something to when it appears in the toilet bowl – from chew to poo – is up to six days; in a healthy body it should be 18 to 24 hours. Check your own transit time by eating sweet corn, sesame seeds or some other identifiable food and then watch for its reappearance in the toilet bowl. If it's more than 24 hours, do something about it.

- We need to look at the packaging of our foods and read the contents. If there are preservatives, colourings, flavourings, hydrogenated fats or numbers listed on the pack, consider replacing it with a natural whole food – that is a food that hasn't had parts of it extracted, processed, recombined or preserved. A good guide is to eat foods that are as close to the way they were grown and harvested, and as free as possible of chemical contaminants. This applies to fruits, vegetables, grains, legumes, seafood, eggs and meats. Whole foods have balanced nutrients that often work synergistically together.

- Margarines were hailed as a healthy alternative to butter because they are low in saturated fats. We know that saturated fats contribute to clogged arteries, which in turn lead to arteriosclerosis, increased cholesterol levels and higher blood pressure. However, if you knew what they have to do to margarine in order for it to have a long shelf life and look like butter, you might think twice before eating it.

- Trans fatty acids are monounsaturated fatty acids that have been changed from their natural state by being chemically hydrogenated – blasted with hydrogen gas after being heated to high temperatures. This makes an oil that has a very long shelf life, which is helpful for the manufacturer but not for the individual consuming it. You'll find these trans fatty acids in anything that says 'hydrogenated fats'.

The fat used in margarine and many other processed foods, including potato chips, hot chips and other fast and junk foods, cake and pancake mixes and most biscuits, are made with these hydrogenated fats. The Institute of Medicine in the US has issued a report stating that there is no safe recommended daily allowance for trans fatty acids and they're being phased out in the US because of law suits. Again, this is an economic decision rather than one based on the health of the consumers.

The problem for the consumers – us – is that the trans fatty acids damage the cell membranes in our bodies and gain easy access to the cell, stopping us from assimilating the good fats and other essential nutrients. When our cells are deprived of energy, we crave refined carbohydrates such as sugar to give ourselves a boost. Refined carbohydrates send our blood sugar levels up, and in response our pancreas pumps out increased insulin levels to bring the blood sugar level down, so we feel fatigued again and reach for the refined carbohydrates once more.

This cycle of increasing our blood sugar through ingesting refined carbohydrates, having it lowered by an increasingly exhausted pancreas and pumping ourselves up again, leads to a risk of diabetes type II, cardiovascular disease, weight gain, hypoglycaemia and many other health disorders. You may be ingesting margarine to help your heart, only to find that the margarine is actually implicated in causing heart disease!

Butter, which has no trans fatty acids, is a far better food for your body than margarine. However, you might want to keep your butter intake to under a couple of teaspoons per day. If you're concerned about the saturated fats in it, then choose a spread made from a combination of oils like olive, sunflower, canola or safflower that contain minimal trans

fatty acids. Better still, use ghee or a cold-pressed oil to dip
bread into.

Ghee contains a balanced ratio of fatty acids and with
none of the trans fatty acids that are so destructive to our
cell membranes. It gives a deliciously rich buttery taste that
allows you to use about half as much as you would if using
oil and it is free of lactose. Ghee is different from clarified
butter in that it has been boiled for a longer period and is
then strained which removes all water and milk fat solids.
This leaves a golden oil which solidifies at room
temperature to a soft solid which is both easy to spread and
has a long shelf life. Ghee has been used for more than
2000 years in Ayurvedic medicine – the ancient healing art
originating in India. It is highly regarded in India as an aid
to promote memory and mental alertness, healthy skin and
good digestion. Ghee can be used in any recipe in place of
butter.

'Cold pressed' means that the manufacturers have
squeezed the oil from the seed rather than heating it to
extract it. This keeps the nutrients intact. High temperatures
change the chemical structure of fats and make them
indigestible and damaging in our body.

- Think about the products you use on your body. Are they
natural and easy for your body to deal with? For instance,
aluminium and chemical preservatives like paraben appear
in the majority of commercially available deodorants. Is the
daily application of aluminium and preservatives into open
pores in our armpits a sensible thing to do? The sweat
glands in our armpits are meant to be draining – that's what
they are there for. Paraben, which is used in many make-up
foundations as well as deodorants, has been shown to be
absorbed into the body. While no direct link has been

established, paraben has been found in many breast cancer samples and it is known to both gravitate to breast tissue and mimic oestrogen in our bodies. I am not suggesting that paraben causes breast cancer in isolation; however, reducing the unnatural chemical load on your body will give it a better chance to process and eliminate unwanted toxins. There are several effective deodorants on the market that don't have aluminium or chemical preservatives amongst their ingredients.

- Cow's milk is a fabulous food – for baby calves. It's enormously rich in nutrients and calcium because a calf, at birth, is skin and bones and then goes through exponential growth where it's laying down massive amounts of calcium throughout its bone structure. We are not laying down a similar bone structure; even young children's bones don't resemble the weight, size or density of cattle bones. Except for domesticated animals, we're the only creatures on the planet who continue drinking milk after we're weaned. The calcium in dark leafy greens and sesame seeds is much easier for our bodies to assimilate than the type found in cow's milk.

  Unless they're born into a cold environment, it is natural for baby mammals to be born 'skin and bones'. This ensures an easy passage into the world for both mother and baby. *Then* a baby grows dramatically because it's fed with its mother's rich milk – perfectly designed for the growth, development and health of that particular species.

We need to think about how we're nourishing our body and see what we might do to improve our nutrition or eating habits. Culturally, we've moved so far away from what is natural and healthy for us that we no longer know how to adequately care for our physical body.

These points are not meant to provide any sort of definitive list of things to avoid or include. That's not my intention. I've mentioned them as foodstuffs we commonly and unthinkingly ingest or use without regard to their long-term appropriateness for our health. If we want our body to serve us well, then we need to take responsibility for how we care for it. Our body serves us 24 hours a day. Even while we sleep it works for us – self-healing, eliminating toxins and dead cells, digesting, processing fresh oxygen, converting nutrients to nourish our cells.

Many people have a problem with their body image, always wanting their body to be different in some way. We complain about cellulite, wrinkles, excess fat, breasts that are too big / too small, our body shape and contours, greying hair, brittle nails – the list goes on. We look disapprovingly in the mirror and heap criticism or despair upon ourselves.

For as long as our happiness is attached to the way our physical body looks, we're destined to ride the eternal merry-go-round of self-criticism / self-congratulation. As we shed a few kilos or improve an aspect of our physical appearance, our confidence soars – only to plummet again when we find something else worthy of our disapproval.

Educate yourself about how your body functions and what it requires for health. Reading books, watching educational programs on health, attending lectures or consulting a naturopath are all good ways to inform yourself about the wonders of your own body and how to provide it with the essentials for health. In this way, you can regain a sense of control over caring for your own body – not as a showpiece, but because it is the temple you inhabit. There are literally thousands of books about healthy nutrition and food preparation, and keeping yourself fit. The Quest for Life Centre is producing a book of recipes that our guests have enjoyed and which are health-enhancing and nutritious.

Mr Duffy lived a short distance away from his body.

James Joyce

There's another very important aspect to your physical body – it is your anchor to the present moment. Your body is always in the present: it's never in the future and it's never in the past. Your mind jumps all over the place – into the future where it projects its hopes, fears, plans; into the past where it regrets, blames, relives, resents, regurgitates.

We tell people to 'come to their senses' when they're caught up in unreasonable thinking. Our body is always here in the present moment and our senses bring us back to what is actually happening. Our minds are full of what isn't – our bodies are immersed in what is.

One of the most effective ways of bringing your mind into the present moment is to connect it with the senses of your body. Right now, as you read, be aware of your posture, your weight, the touch of your clothing against your skin, the pressure of the chair you're sitting on, the floor beneath your feet, the touch of the air caressing your skin, all the sounds within and outside the room in which you sit. Let each breath bring a sense of relaxation, softening any tension held in your body. Let your listening run right out until you hear the clouds passing by. It's impossible to have a fully fledged panic and do this practice at the same time.

The practice of being in the present by connecting with the senses of the body is my most frequent spiritual exercise. By connecting with the senses of the body we experience what's happening right now, rather than have our reality dictated by the mind, which is full of what hasn't happened yet or has already passed. In this way, we begin to live in the world of what is rather than the world of what isn't. We can use the practice of connecting with our senses as a gateway to enlarging our experience of consciousness.

We contribute to our health moment by moment by the quality of our consciousness and the secretion of chemicals in response to the feelings we experience. We can stop secreting the negative stress chemicals of an unmanaged mind preoccupied with the future or past.

We miss out on so much when absorbed by our mind and its chatter. Say we're in a conversation with someone but, in reality, our own internal chatter preoccupies us. This chatter could be our internal dialogue about what the other person is saying or what we think of them but it might equally be about another situation, conversation or event altogether. If we're so absorbed, we're likely to miss their hesitation, emphasis, the fleeting frown that crossed their brow, their shift in posture or any of the other thousand ways by which we communicate in addition to our words.

The richness and depth in our life is found in the present, where we experience the nuances, the exquisiteness, the pure pleasure of being wholeheartedly aware in this moment. When we are present to this moment we can feel the presence of life unfolding around us, of creation coming into being. The feelings engendered by this presence are very different from the ones we feel when our mind is absorbed elsewhere.

Feelings of pure physical joy tingle and ripple through our bodies, creating a cascade of positive health-enhancing chemical benefits as well. This child-like capacity to be fully present to the magic of the moment can be ours, as adults, by conscious choice.

If you watch very young children, say under the age of three, they live very much in the present moment. A child's awareness is captured by whatever she's focused her attention on. If she's making mud pies, she's just making mud pies. She's feeling the texture, wetness, sliminess of the mud; she's probably tasting it, watching it, smelling it and hearing the squelchy sounds it makes as she fashions it into a shape.

She's not half-heartedly making mud pies while fretting over the school years stretching before her. She's simply making mud pies. She may well giggle with glee over her experience of mud.

Young children laugh effortlessly and often because there's a great deal of joy in the present moment. On average, a four-year-old laughs 200 times a day while an adult is lucky to score 15. We squander our capacity to find joy in being present because we're preoccupied by the incessant chatter in our minds.

Apart from laughter providing us with some excellent internal jogging, it also causes our bodies to secrete powerful health-enhancing chemicals. No wonder children's vitality is so much greater than that of most adults.

By listening to our body we begin to get to know it and how it functions. When we live in our body, rather than in our mind, we notice the wonders of our body's functioning. We know when our body feels different from usual. We notice any physical changes that take place. We rejoice in its miraculous work and find joy in its pleasures. We can 'listen' more deeply still to the inner workings of our body and notice fluctuations in our energy level and how our organs are faring.

Not to do so can have dire consequences.

Brian visited me one spring afternoon. He'd just been told he had an inoperable liver cancer and that he'd probably only live another four to six weeks. He couldn't fathom how this could possibly have happened to him – after all, he was in the middle of all kinds of important projects.

Our society places great emphasis and value on intellectual and technological development and this has led to us becoming largely disconnected from the feelings and needs of our physical body. Brian was a man whose mind had been his playground for most of his life. This emphasis on his mental capabilities completely domi-nated him at the expense of his spiritual, emotional and physical aspects. His brilliance and capacity for concentration were renowned. Brian was prolific in his output and was respected widely in his area of expertise.

However, Brian's understanding of his body was less than rudimentary. He knew what he loved to eat and drink and did both with great gusto. He relished long lunches liberally laced with alcohol, which often followed with a dinner party or restaurant meal the same evening.

Brian made no allowance for the fact that his diet and lifestyle might not be conducive to health. The fact that he hadn't noticed that his liver extended from his right groin to under his left rib cage, instead of being tucked under his right ribs, demonstrated his ignorance.

For all his brilliance, Brian didn't have a clue about caring for his physical body and acknowledged with a wry smile that he believed himself to be invincible. His children and partner had also been a casualty of his career pursuits and he lamented his lack of knowing them well or having a close relationship with them. He denied any spirituality, however he was passionate about justice, equality and making a positive difference in people's lives – all of which stem from an awareness of spiritual values.

When he finally came to comprehend how out of balance his life had become, he wept like a baby. Then he set about re-establishing some kind of positive connection with each aspect of himself. Brian lived for several months beyond his doctor's expectations. These precious months saw him heal many of his family relationships. He was able to let those around him know how dear they were to him and he learned to receive the love they held for him.

It is quite common to see people who, on applying many of the principles outlined in this book, but more particularly those in my first two books (*Quest for Life – A Handbook for People with Cancer and Life-Threatening Illness* and *Spirited Women – Journeys with Breast Cancer*), far outlive their doctors' predictions.

These people generally attain a much better quality of life and that leads, in many instances, to an increased quantity of life. Many doctors and cancer specialists now recommend a more holistic approach to the regaining of health. Their advice to their patients to educate themselves in this way is reflected in the increased referrals to our residential programs at the Quest for Life Centre.

The developments in modern medicine have done little to focus our attention on our individual responsibility for the creation of our health. The advent of sulpha drugs and antibiotics led us to believe that the answer to all of humankind's ills would come out of a bottle – that we would find the magic bullet for every disease. This hope stems from the beliefs that nature can be controlled and manipulated without any consequences, and that we can eat and drink what we like and that there will always be some 'magic' to absolve us from our past.

Having recognised the dangers of some of the chemical colourings that have been added to our food, scientists are now isolating the colourings that occur naturally in fruits and vegetables, which are often high in antioxidants. The intention is to then make synthetic chemicals that mimic these naturally occurring colours so that we can add them to other foods. Perhaps children would eat more cauliflower if it were blue ...

Whole organic foods contain a range of vitamins, proteins, enzymes, minerals and micronutrients that work together harmoniously and synergistically. All the individual components are necessary to create a *whole*some food; taking individual components out and recombining them with others is entering uncharted waters.

Many foods – known as 'functional' – are already tampered with in similar ways. There are soft drinks and cereals available with a range of vitamins and stimulants added to them. In time, we'll have vegetables that won't resemble at all their ancient predecessors. Indeed, we will have forgotten what some vegetables and fruits looked like in years past. This will lead to further confusion and lack of trust in our own ability to discern what is healthy and appropriate for us to eat.

It is economic concerns that dictate to the health industry what is acceptable as far as research and development go, and there are few in it who promote the idea of self-responsibility. For instance, and remember that we all have hundreds of genes that may never become activated, medical scientists are now seeking to find the gene 'responsible' for depression. Pharmaceutical companies will then develop a drug to suppress or inactivate that gene. Then the population can be tested and those with the gene can be treated regardless of whether they experience any symptoms of depression or not.

Though a strong argument can be made for this approach, it seems a back-to-front way of looking at health, driven by economics and not based on any interest in consumer health. This premise perpetuates the belief that we're all helpless victims of circumstance with no control over our genetic predispositions. We then seek a higher authority to provide an outer intervention to what is generated within our own body.

There are studies to show that Buddhists and other people who meditate are happier and have less depression, anxiety and physical illness, yet we are generally prescribed medication rather than meditation!

If people were more skilfully assisted to deal with their feelings, we wouldn't secrete the chemicals within our body that *activate* these genetic predispositions. I am concerned, for example, by the large number of people routinely given a drug to help them through the day of their partner's funeral and are then prescribed antidepressants for the ensuing months of grieving. As one recent participant on a Quest for Life Centre program said, 'I want to *feel* the enormity of what has happened to me; not live through this experience in some drug-induced haze.'

Disease is perceived as having an outside cause therefore requiring an outside intervention. Because of this we have fostered a medical system to treat with outside interventions what is often borne of inside causes. We are now overly dependent on experts to whom we hand over our entire decision-making power. Modern-day pills have supplanted the ancient sacred symbol of atonement in the form of communion. We pass the responsibility of our actions to a higher authority outside of ourselves. This modern-day god – modern medicine – is expected to absolve us of our past indiscretions.

I am not denying that there have been many wonderful and useful advances in medicine, but there is a fundamental lack of understanding about what creates or contributes to health and the extraordinary healing powers of our own selves. The health system in the Western world is very sick indeed and the public health system in many areas is in the process of collapse.

Diet

We now recognise that many cancers are caused through eating an inappropriate diet, yet most doctors trivialise the importance of diet to their sick patients. The vast majority of people with cancer are told by their oncologist that what they eat won't make any difference. And when a person has cancer and is underweight, they're encouraged by the hospital dietician to eat ice-cream, cakes, chocolate, milkshakes, biscuits, cream and any other fattening foods they can ingest. This, in my view, is appalling advice to give to someone who's unwell.

Some doctors believe that patients who enquire about diet are doing so because they think there might be a diet that will cure them. In the vast majority of cases, I don't believe this is why a person asks this question. They don't believe a specific diet will fix them, but they're very open to improving their nutrition at a time when it's obvious their health has failed them.

In the tens of thousands of people with cancer and other diseases I've counselled, I've never heard of one specialist who regularly gives any dietary advice to their patients. At best, the patient is told to eat a well-balanced diet which, on probing, couldn't be adequately identified by their specialist. If the patient insists on further information they're referred to the hospital dietician – who generally refers them to the food pyramid which has been turned on its head in the last 30 years.

One of the ways in which we can regain a sense of control over our life is by taking responsibility for our physical health and well-being. And one way to begin is by increasing our knowledge of how to adequately nourish our body.

Your body might have idiosyncrasies due to surgery, illness, trauma or other causes. Through education and by listening to both your body and your intuition, you can tailor a diet that suits your tastes and your lifestyle. Classes on how to prepare healthy food can also be helpful and will expand your ideas about healthy eating.

Be present when you serve yourself food so that you're aware of the amount you're ingesting. Give inward or outward thanks to the person who prepared the food, who planted and harvested it, and who transported it. Eat with appreciation and savour the flavours of the food that you're eating. Stop when your body tells you it's had enough so that you're not satiating an inner unmet need with food.

Make sure you drink plenty of uncontaminated water in your day. Listen to your own body and be guided by it as to quantity. If you're doing a lot of physical, mental or emotional work, then increase your intake of water.

It is better to not drink with your meals so that you allow your body to focus on its job of digestion. Diluting your gastric enzymes and hydrochloric acid with other fluids hastens food out of the stomach before it has been properly digested. You can drink fluids up to 15 minutes before a meal and then, if possible, leave the food undiluted in your stomach for a good hour to an hour-and-a-half after you've eaten.

The exception to this is wine (not spirits). Wine actually stimulates the production of gastric enzymes and hydrochloric acid, so a glass or two of your favourite wine with dinner can be very enjoyable. However, I suggest that you'd benefit from having a couple of alcohol-free days each week.

I'm not suggesting you worry over every morsel that you eat. It's very difficult to ingest a diet of purely whole and organic foods unless you're growing everything yourself and the stress of focusing on every mouthful can be far more detrimental to your health than many of the substances that have found their way into our food supply. I'm suggesting instead that you really think about the way you nourish yourself and endeavour to increase your health through minimising unnecessary additions to a whole-food diet.

Exercise

Our body is designed for movement as much as it is for sitting still. We need to create a balance so that we cooperate with our innate healing forces. We need to fill our body with life-giving oxygen and find exercise that is enjoyable and appropriate to our individual capabilities. If your lifestyle is largely sedentary due to the kind of work you do, then it is important to counterbalance this with enjoyable physical exercise.

Our lymphatic system processes and transports waste material so that it can be eliminated from our body. Unlike the circulatory system that relies on the heart and lungs to pump blood around our body, the lymphatic system depends upon muscular activity to massage the lymphatic fluid throughout channels in our body.

You might find yoga, tai chi or chi gong classes very helpful in using your body in a way that both increases awareness and improves your overall health. Bringing our awareness to simple but precise physical movements helps still the mind and improves circulation, breathing and the secretion of positive health-enhancing chemicals in the brain and other parts of the body.

Likewise, playing sport or exercising vigorously provides us with satisfaction and enjoyment, and has significant cardio-vascular and other health benefits as well.

In times past people were generally more active simply through meeting their physical needs. Whether they did more sweeping, digging, walking, lifting, chopping, winnowing, harvesting or carrying, they *moved* more. Many of these physical activities involved moving the upper part of the body vigorously, which in turn assisted in pumping the lungs, circulating the blood and rotating the thorax area.

Now, many of us sit in front of a computer, our arms and chest moving infrequently, our breasts (male and female) irradiated by computer screens and (for women) held securely in place by underwire bras. (Breasts, like testicles, are meant to move so that blood and lymphatic fluids can circulate freely and without impediment. It lacks commonsense to keep the fatty tissue of our breasts clamped into positions unnatural for them. If you insist on wearing a bra with wire in it, then at least let your breasts wobble freely in your leisure time! Likewise, gentlemen, don't constrict your testicles in tight, uncompromising jeans. Our bits and pieces are meant to jiggle; this keeps them free of sluggishness and encourages the free movement of your lymph and blood circulation.)

If our work requires us to be sedentary then it is essential that we exercise regularly and vigorously in our leisure time. There's sense in the saying, 'If you don't use it, you lose it.'

Breathing

The breath is our connection to life and to consciousness. If you don't breathe, you die. Many people's breathing becomes restricted or shallow when they are under stress. In some of our programs at the Quest for Life Centre, Maureen Williams conducts a breathing relaxation practice that enables participants to settle within themselves and become aware of their breathing. She has contributed the following section on breathing based on her training as an opera singer and as a person who has lived with her own health challenges that have sometimes been life-threatening.

Breathing is a normal, continuous function of the body, which is usually completely unconscious. We should not be able to hear our breathing under normal circumstances and there should be no strain. Shoulders should not rise and fall and the chest should remain almost still. As we breathe in, our stomach will move out slightly. This movement is caused by the diaphragm, or breathing muscle, which is shaped like half a grapefruit and does all the work of breathing. As we speak and use up the air, the diaphragm moves in gradually and smoothly.

The lungs are extremely large organs which give us access to a great amount of oxygen if we use them properly. Paradoxically, if we over-breathe (or hyperventilate) then we get too much oxygen and this is just as ineffective as getting not enough. By learning deep breathing we achieve the right balance of oxygen and carbon dioxide. Continuous shallow breathing means that the air in the bottom of the lungs is not renewed, becomes stale and makes us feel sluggish.

Here is a good way to experience natural deep breathing. Set the alarm for 10 minutes earlier than usual in the morning. Move onto your back, stay relaxed and gently place the palm of your hand on your stomach, just above the navel. Simply become aware of what is happening to your breathing – as you breathe in, your stomach rises, and as you breathe out, it falls. It is as simple as that.

You can expand your breathing with the simple exercises below. When standing, it is important that you have the correct posture and that you are relaxed. If you are tense, the tension is transferred into the rib cage and restricts the amount of air available to you.

Doing each of these exercises several times in sequence, once or twice a day, will heighten your overall awareness of your breathing and how and when you restrict it through holding tension in your body or mind.

Exercise 1 (For Relaxation)

In a standing position, bend your knees slightly and find the position where you feel balanced. Bend forward from the hips, rounding your back, until your head hangs between your knees. Be as floppy as possible. Make sure your neck is relaxed and your head is hanging freely. Return to standing and repeat until you feel relaxed, then move on to Exercise 2.

Exercise 2 (Maintaining Relaxation)

In a standing position, inhale deeply through the nose, then exhale slowly through the mouth. Repeat three times and try to keep the feeling of relaxation you had in the last exercise. Then sigh, allowing your chest to relax further each time. This should open your throat and feel comfortable. Repeat three times.

Exercise 3 (Breathing In)

Breathe in through your nose as if you are smelling something delicious. Hold your breath and keep the rib cage open for five slow counts. Breathe out through the mouth, being aware of your stomach pulling back in. Repeat several times.

Exercise 4 (Breathing In)

Take a deep breath through your mouth as if you are sobbing. Feel the air quickly fill up your chest, making sure that expansion occurs low at the waist. Breathe out and be aware of the ribs springing softly back. Repeat several times.

Exercise 5 (Breathing Out)

Imagine there is a candle about an arm's length in front of your mouth. Inhale through your nose. Hold your breath for three counts, then breathe out quickly through the mouth, as though you're blowing out the candle with a quick rush of air. Repeat several times.

Exercise 6 (Breathing Out)

Breathe in deeply through the nose. Breathe out through your mouth making a hissy 's-s-s-' sound (like air escaping from a balloon). Make the sound smooth and steady and not too loud. Keep your rib cage open as long as you can, then relax it gradually. When you have mastered this exercise, use a clock to time your exhalations. Repeat and try to improve your time.

Being conscious of your breathing draws you back into the present moment. If you are tense or distracted, using Maureen's breathing practices can help you settle and refocus.

Sleep Issues

We seem to be cramming more and more things into our days and nights, often at the expense of our need for adequate rest. Ours is a culture that soldiers on with little regard for replenishing ourselves through rest and sleep. We even talk about diseases in terms of hospital 'bed nights'; a surgical procedure will require so many 'bed nights' if all goes to plan. The idea of convalescence, indeed even the word, has disappeared. Yet convalescence – when they popped a blanket over our knees and parked us in front of a window so that we could stare into the distance – enabled us to physically rest and recover, and to mentally, emotionally and spiritually take on board what had just happened to us physically. Convalescence gave us the opportunity to review, reassess and grow in wisdom and understanding – taking that wisdom with us into the future. Now, we want people upright and back at the workplace or functioning as quickly as possible, allowing no adequate time to rest, replenish, incorporate, integrate and learn from the experience of illness.

It generally takes us several hours to drift down through the levels to reach deep sleep, where our brain waves create the deepest physical rest and when our body does most of its healing and repair work. It's also where children do most of their growing. If we're physically, mentally or emotionally upset or in pain we may not access our deep sleep level. Sleeping medication doesn't allow us to naturally access this deep sleep level, and that's why we seldom wake from a medicated slumber feeling refreshed and revitalised.

I've met many people for whom sleep only comes when it overtakes them in front of their television sets. They don't consciously choose to go to sleep; they wait for unconsciousness to overtake them while they're doing something else. These people would benefit from consciously going to sleep in their beds at a time of their choosing.

A good night's sleep makes any day seem more manageable. If you find it hard to get a good night's sleep, try the following suggestions. You might need to follow all of the suggestions for at least a week before you begin to see the benefits of your efforts.

- Make an absolute commitment to yourself that you will not 'think things through' in the middle of the night as you know it's the most unproductive time for coming up with solutions to problems. If you can't sleep or can't get back to sleep, put a time limit on how long before you get up, make yourself a cuppa, read something or put in place some other strategy for not letting your mind run the show. Using one of the sleep practices mentioned below might be helpful.

    Of course, you may be an exception – some people have

periods of great clarity and productivity in the middle of the night. Listen to what is right for you, but do not settle for restless or tormented thinking.

- You might find sleeping with the window open to let in fresh air helpful, no matter what the season.

- Sleep in natural fibres such as cotton, wool or silk. Natural fibres allow your body to breathe. This applies to both your bedding and sleepwear.

- Avoid eating for at least one-and-a-half hours before going to sleep otherwise your body will be too busy with the process of digestion and your sleep will be disturbed.

- Avoid sugars (at all times) and other stimulants like coffee before sleeping – they make your nervous system jittery.

- Avoid doing anything too vigorous just before sleep, unless it involves making love. The chemicals of loving are conducive to peaceful sleep and going to sleep with a smile on your face leads to sweeter dreams! Otherwise, do exercise earlier in the day as it mobilises your metabolism.

- Have a warm bath or shower before going to bed. This relaxes and soothes your body and distributes your blood to the peripheral capillaries. Make showering or bathing a ritual by imagining the day's stresses being washed from your body and mind.

- Use an aromatherapy candle or perfumed oil to establish an association between that particular perfume and going to sleep.

- De-clutter your bedroom to de-clutter yourself. For example, put fresh sheets on the bed, clear dressers or furniture of discarded clothing and put shoes away. Create a soothing sleeping environment.

- Using a herbal relaxant can be helpful. Herbs don't make you sleepy but they help to nourish your nervous system. Ask your pharmacist or health food storeowner for a recommended formula.

- Have plenty of uncontaminated water in your diet and drink most of it in the earlier part of the day.

- Spend 10 minutes reviewing your day *before* you get into your night attire or bed. At that time, bring your body to rest in the present, then revisit conversations and activities, and make a note of anything forgotten or overlooked / misunderstood that needs revisiting tomorrow. Writing it down consciously enables you to switch off the mind more easily when you go to bed.

- Read something inspirational before you settle down to sleep, or perhaps keep a 'blessing book' by your bed. Write down five things to be grateful for before you go to sleep. This trains the mind to identify and focus on the positive aspects of your life.

- Consider using a relaxation or 'sleep practice' as you drift off to sleep, to keep the mind disciplined rather than randomly thinking. A relaxation practice will take you straight to your deep sleep level where you'll access your deepest healing rest. I've made one called *Sleep* available on CD which many people find helpful in attaining deep, refreshing sleep.

- Have a tape or CD ready to play if you waken during the night. If you do, go to the bathroom, go back to bed and start the tape or CD before your mind becomes active.

- Learn some relaxation techniques and practise them during the day to familiarise yourself with the experience of being physically relaxed.

- Create a sacred space for yourself where you can spend some quiet time and internally de-clutter yourself. It might be in a room or at a table or in a corner where you like to meditate, keep treasures from your walks, do your inspirational reading, and place fresh flowers, a peace candle, poetry, treasures from children in your life. Make it a place you return to in your spirit to refresh, uplift and inspire yourself.

- Consider having a massage every week or two to assist your body to relax if you're going through an emotionally challenging time or your body is holding a lot of physical tension.

Fluffing Yourself Up

'Fluffing up' your body means to give it pleasure. Get to know what your body loves – massage, hugs, caresses, manicures, beauty, music, fresh flowers, pedicures, spas, facials, aromatherapy, making love – and make sure you have enough of these things to enable your body to feel cared-for and fabulous. Giving your body pleasure releases many powerful and health-enhancing chemicals and hormones. Feeling fabulous is not just a state of mind; it's a state of physiology. Our body secretes powerful immune-enhancers and other beneficial chemicals when we feel physical pleasure.

Your body has an innate driving force for healing; it is the strongest force within your body. Your body is where the spiritual, emotional and mental aspects come together and are reflected in health. As you learn to listen deeply to your body you begin to understand what is in need of healing within you – whether that is an attitude or belief, a judgement, an unmet need or an unexpressed feeling. By cooperating with the healing mechanism within your body and giving it the ingredients for health, it will serve you well.

Our bodies enjoy sensual pleasures and need them for optimum health and vitality. Make time to enjoy the perfume of flowers; to watch the changing colours of the sunset; to swim in the sea or a river or lake; to listen to birdsong and music; to savour the taste of fresh, simple foods; to follow a wave to the shore, the ripple into stillness; to receive a hug, a caress or a massage.

Sometimes we're at war with our body and are so bent on controlling it, or its physical appearance, that we forget to enjoy the simple things that give us such pleasure. Learn to listen to your body and respectfully give it what it enjoys.

It is your responsibility to learn how to nourish, rest, exercise and fluff up your body. It is a living creation that you can honour and support with knowledge and appropriate care. By focusing on the ingredients for a healthy lifestyle, you create the ideal environment for your body.

What goes on in our mind also affects the functioning of our body. Our beliefs dictate our actions and our life unfolds accordingly. Once awareness dawns on our potential to change beliefs, the path opens before us to transform our life.

CHAPTER 5

Beliefs Matter

---

*It is not about being right – there are no 'right'
answers, unless our goal is to perpetuate a belief.*

Me

Your life is a perfect reflection of your beliefs.

Andrew Mathews

*What you intend in your thoughts with passion,
you will act upon and ultimately create.*

Wayne Dyer

*If it doesn't mirror some part of myself, I cannot
see it.*

Me

*Our goal is not to change the world or even
ourselves.*
*Our goal is to change our perceptions about the
world and about ourselves.*

Paul Ferrini

Beliefs, attitudes, values, assumptions, expectations and judgements are all within our mind. Our mind holds our basic
philosophy of how life should be lived, even how it should unfold.

For instance, we might believe that if we're honest and trust-worthy then life will deal with us fairly. If someone then treats us badly, we're confronted with our feelings about having that belief challenged. This triggers related feelings from past experiences and they, in turn, may bring a whole litany of other thoughts and feel-ings in train. Indulge the following tale as a mundane example of what happens moment by moment in our lives.

Imagine you're standing in a crowd at a food stall. Someone is quietly but persistently pushing to get in front of you. Perhaps your mind reacts by telling you that this isn't how people should behave. You took on this belief unconsciously as a child because that is what you were told or from subsequent experiences that left you wounded in some way. Perhaps this came about through someone getting his or her needs met at your expense.

You've created or maintained the belief because if you (and everyone else – and therein lies the hornet's nest) live by it, you'll protect yourself from ever being wounded in this way again. So, in this case, believing that people should wait their turn reassures us that our needs will be met.

The problem is, not everyone shares our belief. These beliefs often cover a very vulnerable place inside ourselves and it's likely that we'll feel quite defensive around them. A telltale sign of a belief covering an unhealed emotional wound is when we feel defensive or prickly when it's questioned.

The situation that prompted this reaction – the defensiveness or prickliness – can be perceived as a threat or as an opportunity. The mind will see it as a threat to its cherished beliefs – its job is to maintain the beliefs we've adopted and our inner antenna is con-stantly scanning for evidence to support them. We see what our awareness focuses on.

Say I believe I'm inferior to other people. If a stranger across the street gives me a grouchy look, my mind may well see that as support for my belief. In the next moment, I've taken it personally and I might even feel attacked by this stranger when the fact is she had an argument with her boyfriend that morning and she's still feeling grumpy with herself and him. She probably hasn't noticed me at all and, if she has, she's probably too caught up in her own misery to be bothered with me anyway.

In truth, such beliefs are not a threat to *you* because consciousness is beyond threat. To your mind's beliefs, painstakingly collected to protect an emotional wound of the past, such beliefs may *feel* very threatening. As discussed in Chapter 1, Welcome to the Planet, we are 'feeling' beings long before we are 'thinking' beings. Such present-time encounters elicit stored reactions – reactions – in our brain and body. Through the repetition of a feeling in our earlier life we activate areas of the brain, which in turn build a particular belief to explain or name, the feeling.

For instance, looking at the above example, if in childhood, we had many experiences in which we felt less than other people, inferior to other people, not as good as other people or that our efforts would not be as productive as other people then we electrically activate, through the production of neurotransmitters, a particular group of cells in the brain. We continue to re-activate this neural network in our brain because it is familiar to us, it has been our experience up until now, it is what we expect from the present moment and we anticipate that the future will continue to bring us the same re-actions.

In the same way, some people cultivate thoughts of being superior to other people because they too, have been wounded by life and are protecting a vulnerable feeling within themselves. These people need to reassure themselves by believing they are better than, are superior to, are more capable than, other people. Feeling superior to other people is the flip-side of feeling inferior. Both states of mind serve to make us feel separate from one another yet everything in us yearns for unity, wholeness and the experience of being at one with ourselves and our world.

We are bound by these habitual re-actions until something happens to change our view of the world. We might hope that things will change, that we will feel less inferior or superior in time, but hoping will bring no change unless it is backed up by conscious choice.

This conscious choice means that we now have the possibility to activate a different neural network in our brain.

The brain has 100 billion nerve cells. It contains a smorgasbord of possibilities. We are moulded by our early experiences and the feelings they elicit. Different areas of the brain are activated according to the repeated experience of feelings. If we feel secure in the love that is shown to us, that we have our place within the family and ultimately the community, that our needs are met, that we are valued simply because we exist and, in time, that we build confidence in our ability to meet the challenges that come our way, then we could say that this is the seed of self-esteem. From a neuroscientific perspective, it could be said that self-esteem is the repeated activation of a particular neural network in the brain, the chemical consequences of which affect every cell of our body.

When our consciousness is absorbed by a group of thoughts, we activate corresponding neural activity in the brain. In this lies the possibility of changing our experience of reality. We are not programmed or destined to helplessly re-act. Human beings have the capacity to direct their consciousness. We can change the focus of our consciousness by choice. We don't know that we have choice until we do. We continue to re-activate our past experiences until something causes us to ponder whether there might be another possible response.

In light of this, every reaction we experience can be an opportunity for us to choose a more appropriate response.

However, back to the food stall. Hot on the heels of life's challenge to your belief that people should wait their turn, come the feelings stirred by this belief plus any related thoughts. For instance, if my self-esteem is poor, I might react by thinking, 'She hasn't even noticed I'm here', or 'She has noticed me and she doesn't care. Everyone acts as if they're more important than I am. Maybe they are. Maybe I *am* just a nobody. I feel like a nobody.'

Alternatively, if I've figured out that anger effectively gets my needs met, then I might react by saying to the person who's pushing in, 'Hey, you! Watch what you're doing! I was here first,' and back up my aggressive stance with body language to match.

If I've been to assertiveness-training classes to recover my self-esteem, I might say, 'Excuse me. I notice that you're nudging your way in front of me even though I was here first. Would you mind waiting your turn?'

Or if I've been raised in a household where feelings were never acknowledged or appropriately expressed, I may find myself simply stewing in my own head: 'I hate people who push in front of me. It always happens. I never get what's due to me. Who does she think she is? She looks like a real loser anyway.' I might continue to fume and fester with these unexpressed emotions until I'm finally served. Then I find myself ordering a double-malted chocolate milkshake hoping it will help me feel better emotionally when really I only set out to get a mineral water in the first place.

The roller-coaster ride of mind and emotions continues. The powerlessness, the justifications, the hurt, the despair, recriminations, the anger – even rage, the indignation, feelings of failure and the judgements circle and swoop on relentlessly.

We are rarely angry or upset for the reasons we think. We can all remember an experience when we reacted out of all proportion to the stimulus. We're not just feeling the upset caused by someone pushing in front of us. We're dealing with our unhealed emotional history around feeling 'I won't get my needs met', 'I haven't got what it takes', 'I have to be pushy to get anywhere', 'I don't matter' or whatever the belief might be.

Looking to the physical world for the satisfaction of our inner needs is the cause of much of our distress and fear. We fear any changes in our circumstances because we believe this will deprive us of peace. We might fear losing our job or our partner because we believe that our life cannot give us peace without these two essentials.

We might be at pains to make our life look terrific to everyone else because we can't bear people – even ourselves – knowing we're not really happy. So we strive to gather the toys of affluence in the hope that they'll bring us satisfaction and will serve to demonstrate our success in life. We may fear telling the truth because we think other people might not like us for it. We fear the future because of its uncertainty. We fear the past because it might be repeated. Fear may become our usual state as we find our mind leaping from past to future thus depriving us of the opportunities that exist in the present.

Many of our daily fears don't even seem substantial enough to be called fears. Becoming the constant chatter in our heads, these 'concerns' niggle at us as we weigh up everything that happens to us. Will I get it right? Should I do that or this? What if they don't approve of me? Should I try again? What if xyz happens? How will I cope?

We may feel the victim of these concerns and fears as they influence or indeed, dictate, our choices and decisions in life. Most of us try to conceal their presence from other people as no-one enjoys admitting their vulnerabilities. If we feel disturbed or overwhelmed by our concerns or fears they may also emerge in our dreaming when our unconscious mind endeavours to make sense of our experiences.

Creating a safe, non-judgemental environment for ourselves can allow us to explore and understand ourselves more deeply. With a compassionate understanding of ourselves comes the possibility for new choices and new decisions.

More and more people are using drugs, alcohol or prescribed medication to quell their fears and anxieties simply because they don't know a better way of managing them. The doctors in our communities are increasingly depended upon to do counselling work with their patients and yet they're pressured by the medical economic system to see as many patients in a day as possible. 'Six-minute medicine' is promoted – literally meaning that the average consultation should be able to be conducted in the space of six minutes! Prescribing a pharmaceutical drug to alleviate anxiety is an easier and quicker way to manage patients than listening to their stories and offering practical strategies that will assist them in dealing with their anxieties more effectively. Many doctors are like-wise seeking to manage their own unresolved emotional history and may or may not be helpful to their patients depending on their knowledge and comfort around certain issues.

There was a time, long ago, when the role of a doctor was to teach people about the ingredients for health and healing. Now doctors study and treat disease with little emphasis or focus on the creation of health and healing. This has come about largely due to technological and surgical advances and the development of the pharmaceutical industry. The economics of listening deeply to patients doesn't stack up against the profits to be made from people who stay stuck with unresolved emotions that can be suppressed through medication. This is gradually changing at some universities, as this deeper understanding of the healing relationship between doctor and patient is recognised. As Dr Rachel Naomi Remen said so eloquently:

The reality is that healing happens between people. The wound in me evokes the healer in you, and the wound in you evokes the healer in me, and then the two healers collaborate.

In my private counselling practice as well as in our residential programs at the Quest for Life Centre, doctors often speak with great sadness, even despair, about their disappointment that the care they provide to their patients has been reduced to this 'six-minute medicine' model.

I would suggest that the sole purpose of human existence is to relinquish everything that stops us from experiencing full awareness of our own consciousness. Life continues to bring us experiences, including illnesses, as opportunities to release ourselves from a limiting view of our true nature – pure consciousness.

Just as our body has an innate knowledge about healing itself, so our consciousness naturally seeks to express itself in its fullness. We can co-operate with this process by relinquishing the limiting beliefs that we have adopted in our life. When you cut yourself, you don't have to worry about how to get white blood cells to the wound or how to send fibrin and collagen to begin the process of healing. You may need to create an appropriate environment for healing by cleaning the wound or having it stitched. However, the healing of the wound is a natural response of the body to re-establish the integrity of the skin and underlying tissue. Likewise, consciousness seeks the full expression of itself by creating opportunities to release what is not true of its essence.

Just as we might need to create the environment for our body to heal itself, so too we may need to create an appropriate environment for this emotional healing.

If we don't see limiting beliefs for what they are – a bandage over some emotional wound – and if we don't have the courage and willingness to choose a different response to the presence of such beliefs in our lives, we will continue to live with our unhealed emotions. We will continue to foist the past onto the present and in this way repeat our history and secure a similar future.

If our consciousness is absorbed by fears, limiting beliefs, judgements, likes and dislikes then the reality we experience is dictated by those states of mind and the chemical consequences that our brain and body secrete in response. Our brain and body are in constant communication through the secretion of neuropeptides, hormones, neuro-transmitters and other chemicals that influence the functioning of our organs. Our emotional reactions, and the feelings that flow from them, are embedded into the tissues of our bodies through these chemicals.

If we're forever caught up in negative self-talk – an internal critic continually commenting on our performance and undermining our peace – then life is going to seem like a struggle where we constantly feel we don't have what it takes to meet its challenges. No matter what opportunities present themselves, we'll only perceive them according to our negative view of the world. We'll look for the flaw, for the reason why the opportunity is actually a threat to our sense of security. We'll see exactly why it won't work for us and argue the point passionately.

We argue against an opportunity passionately because we're working to cover an emotional wound we either find too painful or too difficult to resolve. Or because there's some kind of mileage in hanging on to such undermining thoughts. After all, we say to ourselves, if I never take a risk, I'll never fail. If I don't heal myself of limiting beliefs, then I won't have to aim too high. And, sadly, we make life decisions based on such thought processes, and then have to live by the consequences.

However, it doesn't serve our highest purpose, or the world's, to hide the light of our consciousness under a bucket of negativity borne of unhealed emotional wounds. The world needs all the light it can get right now, and our clarity, peace, humour and wisdom is essential to us if we want to live our lives skilfully. If we are a living demonstration of those qualities in our family, they, and our community and the wider community of the planet, will benefit from our presence.

Someone wrote some beautiful words along the lines of, 'When you were born you were crying and everyone around you was smiling. Live your life so that when you die you are smiling and everyone around you is crying.'

So often our awareness is absorbed by the mind's chatter about our perceived future or unchangeable past or some form of inner criticism. Watch how often during the day, while you're going about your daily routine, your mind is either already on the next task or has wandered elsewhere altogether.

An unchecked mind robs us of peace because peace is a present-time feeling. So if the mind drags us away from the present and dwells on negative perceptions and judgements, that will be our experience of reality, moment by moment, and will contribute to our biology and health.

It is in the minutiae of our daily lives that we have the opportunity to observe the judgements we hold in our minds. Our reactions to events and situations speak volumes about the judgements we habitually hold. With awareness we can challenge and release the judgements that don't serve the purpose mentioned earlier – to relinquish limiting beliefs.

Imagine we're walking down the street and we see a mother hit her toddler with more force than she'd wished. Our natural tendency could be to respond with compassion for the child, who's feeling confused, frightened and is suffering; and for the mother, who has been driven to such resorts believing it's the only way to re-establish control. The mother's suffering is etched into her face, shows in her rigid body, resonates in the sound of her voice and controls her gestures. We see the chemical consequences of her feelings eloquently expressed in every part of her body.

We are present to her distress and our heart opens in compassion, allowing us to understand the feelings of the young mother. We remember some situation in our own life when we felt helpless and wanted to lash out; an echo of the agony of spinning helplessly, our whole life out of control. And we understand the compassion and courage necessary to embrace our own helplessness and fear, allowing it to find its rest within us.

In this scenario, when I say 'we remember some situation in our life when we felt helpless', I mean that we literally re-member; in that moment, we 'bring together' in our mind or re-activate the memory of how it feels to be in that place because we have observed it within ourselves. If we judge ourselves harshly for having such feelings, we will also project that judgement onto other people who we see behaving similarly. However, when we have embraced our wounded self with compassionate forgiveness, we are able to greet the mother with a gentler heart.

Our eyes meet and, in so doing, convey a shared understanding of this woman's suffering and our remembering of some greater aspect of ourselves that is beyond this immediate distraction. A fleeting smile passes, and in that precious moment peace descends amidst the screaming and the upset as we experience a moment of being at one with each other. She, like us, is doing the best she knows how to, with her life. And without so much as a word being uttered we move on, feeling nourished by a sacred moment of connection.

Compassion is our natural state when we relinquish the judgements we hold about ourselves and other people. These judgements are literally 'held' in our brain and body by the neural network created by our re-action to an emotional wound. Compassion is an innate quality of pure consciousness. Compassion melts all barriers of class, ethnicity, wealth or lack of it, social standing, sexual orientation or educational background. Life is simply a drama unfolding around us. What we make of it is up to us.

If we haven't healed the emotional wounds of our history, we are likely to re-act – to act again – from our judgements. If we want peace to be our experience, then we need to bring our awareness to our re-actions and, in so doing, we have the opportunity to choose a more appropriate response; we exert response-ability. If we have relinquished our judgements through compassionate understanding and forgiveness, the same situation can elicit a response from us rather than an habitual re-action.

In our story of the young mother for example, if we have a history rich with wounds that justify protective beliefs, we might have closed our heart and heaped judgement upon her in our mind, shooting her a withering look like an arrow meant to wound, and perhaps feeding upon her misery and shame again later by repeating the tale to a friend: 'Do you know what I saw today? This woman beating her kid for no good reason. People like her shouldn't be allowed to have kids. I felt like giving her a whack to show her how it feels.' Needless to say, this kind of thinking leads only to a perpetuation of the problem of feeling helpless and wanting to lash out.

Yet all these feelings and judgements have nothing to do with the distraught young mother. Our encounter with her – and indeed every encounter – provides a mirror to our reactions, beliefs and the judgements that would close our hearts and separate us from any sense of spiritual connection. Judgement always separates; that is its function.

The accumulation of unexpressed feelings from past emotional wounds lies open and present in the brain, creating a neural network of chemical and electrical activity. Our beliefs protect our wounded feelings and attempt to justify their existence. These beliefs, and the judgements that flow from them, are 'second nature' to us. We use a considerable amount of energy to maintain the intricate structure of beliefs necessary to protect the wounded emotional being. This is nearly always done unconsciously, though we can also make life-changing decisions based on beliefs we've installed around a very painful event.

Our unresolved feelings, resulting from emotional wounds, become chemically and electrically activated in our brain and body when we experience reactions to present time events. We can choose to see these re-actions as an opportunity to heal. As we bring the light of our compassion and understanding to these feelings and allow their expression in healthy ways, we release ourselves from our re-actions.

We yearn to experience our first nature; pure consciousness untainted by wounds, judgements and reactions. These neural networks held in the brain, and which constantly affect the functioning of our body, are released, as we heal the emotional wounds of the past.

The experience of union has been the impetus for spiritual seekers throughout history. Science and spirituality have arrived at a common understanding though the implications of this understanding are yet to be clearly articulated. The implications of this understanding will, in time, change the way we conduct ourselves individually, as families, communities and as nations. Science uses one language, spirituality uses another.

Why wouldn't the blissful experience of union be every bit as physical as it is profoundly spiritual? These moments of blissful union can now be witnessed when the brain is scanned. When a person is immersed in a state of loving consciousness, brain scanning shows great electrical activity in the left frontal lobe of the brain. It is in this state of pure consciousness that we feel the profound experience of union. Pure consciousness experiences its own presence in everything. The physical experience of love, joy and bliss have profound impacts on our health through the beneficial secretion of hormones such as oxytocin, anandamide and others, yet to be named and understood.

The unresolved feelings we experience are a constant call to our compassion so that we might experience this union. We can allow our hearts to embrace the fear, the rage, the emptiness or whatever it is that ails us. Then, once our tears are no more, we can consider what, if anything, needs to be done to allow the emotion's passage into our history.

Some people find benefit in creating a ritual of release, in some symbolic way, to signify a new way of being in the world. For instance, this might involve the lighting of candles or incense, the burning of paper on which painful emotions and beliefs have been written, the planting of trees or a garden, the relinquishing of possessions no longer needed, a visit to a physical place that means something to the individual or a conversation with someone with whom we had an issue. In this last example, the person with whom you had an issue may no longer be alive or physically present in your life. This is no reason not to have the conversation, or you can write a letter to them if you prefer. You might choose to set up a chair for the person and read your letter to them, or say what is in your heart now that you're willing to release the emotional trauma that lay between you. The person doesn't need to be present or aware of what you are doing because this act of release is not about the other person over whom you have no control; you do this practice for yourself, to release yourself from the wounds of the past.

Once we're aware of our wounded emotions and the beliefs we've fostered around them, we have a choice. But until awareness dawns we're destined to simply react. If we refuse to heal, then we sacrifice the peace that's possible in the present, because fear and love can never be experienced in the same moment. The choice to fear or to love always awaits us, yet we need to be present and aware to make the choice. Through awareness we find forgiveness and this leads to an ability to see that nothing wrong is happening; then we can choose to bring love to the situation rather than fear.

We all know people who use what's happened to them in the past as an excuse for how they are in the present. If we're honest, we'll see the same thing within ourselves. We know people (and we might be one of them!) who say, 'It's just the way I am!' This is a wonderful excuse to remain stuck! Rest assured, the bluster around such a statement means that we're protecting a part of ourselves that feels it has been emotionally wounded in the past. Many people use anger, moodiness or sulkiness as a way of protecting a part of themselves they don't know how to heal. It is sometimes easier to stay feeling wounded than to embrace the challenge that leads to healing.

The beliefs, and the judgements that stem from them, are held in our mind – and brain – and will justify their own existence, demanding that we see them as right and necessary. Yet, it is not about being right. There are no 'right' answers unless our goal is to perpetuate a belief. If the belief no longer serves our heightened awareness, then holding onto it only perpetuates our re-actions.

If we want peace more than anything, it is helpful to stop labelling things as good or bad, right or wrong. Think instead in terms of behaviours and attitudes that are more or less useful in our journey towards greater peace and heightened awareness. This perspective removes the judgement against ourselves, other people, events and situations. We shift from having our reality dictated by that which is happening *outside* of ourselves to that which is taking place *within* ourselves. With this awareness comes choice. Without this awareness we are destined to react habitually.

Thinking in these terms, we can perceive attitudes and behaviours in ourselves, our family, our community and our nation as more or less useful in the creation of peace; a habit or belief is not 'wrong' – it's just not useful to maintain if we want peace in our life. This is far more than a matter of semantics. It involves a fundamental shift in perspective that is essential if we are to live from the inside out, rather than having our reality dictated to us by outside events.

As I discussed previously, some people awaken to a rainy day to find that they're miserable because they believe rainy days are miserable ones. Others will awaken with a smile at hearing the patter of rain on the roof and leap out of bed to go forth and embrace the day. If peace is our priority, we might want to question our belief about rainy days, shift our perspective and adopt a sunny inner disposition without regard to the weather. The rain just rains; how we feel about the rain, that's up to us.

This is where flexibility, resilience and compassion for ourselves enter the equation. Fresh insights and healing won't occur if we're rigidly holding onto beliefs only because they're familiar and habitual, without questioning their relevance to each new situation. Sometimes staying stuck with our suffering because it's familiar seems easier than taking a leap of faith into the unknown. It *can* feel like stepping off the edge and falling into the abyss that yawns before us because we feel vulnerable when we let go familiar patterns of behaviour, even when it involves suffering. Yet, what else is there to do between now and death but to liberate ourselves from the suffering that would keep us bound to the past?

When beliefs borne of our suffering continue in our unconscious, we also overlay them onto the present. In this way we continue to recreate our history because we can only perceive the present through the lenses of the beliefs we have gathered to protect ourselves – just as we did at the food stall, when we didn't approach this new situation with an openness and contentment, but with the historical beliefs we hold about ourselves: 'I don't get my needs met', 'I have to be first', 'Life's not fair to me', 'I'm unworthy of respect' or whatever. In fact, we might already be unconsciously on alert when a situation has the potential to bring us grief; we start to get stressed even before we've encountered the event – and in the extreme may even choose not to participate in life because we feel continually thus thwarted.

We usually don't possess the necessary objectivity to see that the other person in a scenario like the one at the food stall is likewise acting from their belief and, needless to say, holds their view of the world to be right.

If we cultivate such objectivity, the same scene could be experienced quite differently. We might notice the behaviour of the other person and respond by letting them in ahead of us. We might feel quite content in the knowledge that all our needs will be met, that we're happy to be who and where we are and, on observing this person's behaviour, are able to accommodate their need to be first. After all, would we rather be right or happy?

As for the 'intruder' at the food stall, she might have emerged from a childhood where the only way she got her needs met was by being pushy. It's not personal: we might simply be the obstacle she expects to have to overcome in her way of doing things, and so unconscious might she be to this pattern, she doesn't even notice that we're anything more than her 'obstacle'.

So, if we take her actions personally, as a direct affront against us, we can add this experience to our storehouse of grievances, and the next time a similar event takes place, we'll have even more weapons with which to bolster our fundamental belief – that people should wait their turn.

The problem with this belief and all its consequences is that they're based on unhealed feelings from past experiences. The wounds of the past continue to affect us in the present until they're brought to our consciousness and are healed.

Healing happens when we acknowledge our feelings and whole-heartedly embrace them. Through the regular practice of meditation, for example, we can witness these feelings and not be overwhelmed by them. We grow when we can witness these unhealed patterns from the past and choose to *respond* appropriately rather than *react* unconsciously.

With awareness we can either witness our feelings or find safe and appropriate ways to express them in a manner that doesn't wound ourselves or other people. In this way, we release ourselves from their influence. This is the essence of forgiveness – to let go of the pain of our resistance to what is. Forgiveness is not about condoning the behaviour. Yet we may well be able to find the heart to forgive the *being* without condoning the *behaviour*.

I know I could still be sitting in the cave outside of Assisi at the monastery I'd retreated to when I had leukaemia, feeling sad and sorry for myself. I could still be muttering quietly to myself, 'It's not fair. I didn't deserve to grow up with my complex brother Brenden. He shouldn't have told me before we were ten years old that he had to take his own life by the time he was 30. I shouldn't have had to spend my teen years in hospital having my legs surgically rearranged. I shouldn't have been raped. I shouldn't have gotten into drugs. I shouldn't have had to live with the feeling of impending doom that Brenden's life had instilled in me. He shouldn't have killed himself. My husband shouldn't have left me stranded with two small children in another country. It's not fair that I now have leukaemia and will probably die.'

Indeed, I could probably have gathered together a fan club of people who would have supported me in my misery – people who would have agreed wholeheartedly and said, 'Yes, Petrea, you stay in that little cave just as long as you want because all those things should never have happened to you! It's not fair. You didn't deserve it and it's terrible that all those things happened. You stay feeling miserable just as long as you want to.'

But would that have changed anything? The fact is, those things *had* happened. Was I going to allow the events of my history define who I was? Or could I be more than that? Could I create enough heart to contain the pain and anguish of the past without losing the capacity to love? Or was I going to allow my past to diminish and embitter me as a human being? That was the challenge. Now I feel incredibly blessed because of the opportunities life has given me.

I wouldn't wish the events of my life on anyone else. However, how can I be grateful for who I am now unless I accept the journey that has brought me to this place? Indeed, I am grateful for those experiences because they have broken me open to compassion in a way that was unlikely to have happened if my life had been without suffering. I am a better companion to other people who likewise suffer, because I am no longer fearful of the feelings that suffering brings.

Beliefs and Feelings

Some years after I emerged from the cave and was at an Attitudinal Healing conference in San Francisco where Dr Jerry Jampolsky was speaking on the topic of forgiveness, a six-foot-five transsexual in a frock stood up and in a deep voice said, 'I've just realised! Forgiveness is giving up all hopes for a better past.' And I understood exactly what that meant for me.

When our belief system is shattered we feel personally attacked and react emotionally.

Until forgiveness appears as an option, we might live with feelings of anger, resentment, powerlessness, blinding rage or bitterness, or thoughts of revenge. Or depression might settle as a blanket of impotence and inertia over all the unresolved feelings as we flounder helplessly against the past.

We can see in a person's face the judgements and the consequent emotions that visit there regularly. Have you not seen bitterness etched into someone's face? Stubbornness long-held in a jaw? Laughter lines around the eyes in a person who finds joy in living? Defeat or failure weighing down upon someone's stooped shoulders?

In this way, in every moment, we contribute to our physical health. These states of mind – and physiology – also influence how much and what we choose to eat and our lifestyle habits, and these, in turn, contribute to our physical health. And so the consequences of our beliefs, feelings and choices are translated into our physical body.

The shattering of a dearly held belief can be profoundly distressing – especially when we're convinced our belief is right.

I've seen numbers of men in particular who, within three to 12 months of shattering a fundamental belief, have developed cancer. One such man was Greg.

Greg had a varied and successful business career built on honesty and integrity, both of which he valued highly. His family ties were close and he sat on several boards where his experience and expertise were valued. Greg and his wife, Helen, shared everything and were obviously happy.

Greg's trust in life and his expectation that people would treat him honourably had never been seriously challenged in his adult life. He believed he'd long left behind the emotional pain experienced in his early youth when his father had unexpectedly left the family home and moved in with the nextdoor neighbour, only to die shortly after. The fact that this had happened at a time when Greg was forming his ideas and beliefs about sex, relationships, life and his place in the world made the situation all the more challenging.

Two years before Greg and I met, a friend from his school years, Tom, had reappeared in his life. He and Tom had found some common interests that led to a business affiliation and the creation of a company. Greg had planned to retire in the near future and he could see that milestone on the horizon with such a profitable enterprise in the offing.

When it came to the finer details of tying down their business arrangement, Tom was preoccupied with other matters. Greg was keen to finalise their agreement in writing – a practice he'd long adhered to – but Tom slapped him on the shoulder and said there was no need for an agreement. They'd known each other since they were kids, Tom maintained, and why would they need to fuss about an agreement when they were best mates? According to Tom, there was plenty of time to sort out those kinds of details. What they needed to do was make some decisions about warehousing the stock that was soon to arrive.

Greg didn't feel right about the way in which Tom worked but could see the value in focusing on getting the business underway – there were significant profits to be made. Then Greg experienced another moment of not feeling right about Tom's business practices. Though nothing was said, Greg realised that Tom had in fact ordered this stock long before their reacquaintance and, as it transpired, didn't have funds available when the shipment arrived. He fobbed Greg off with excuses about his money being freed up in a few weeks. And when the shipment arrived earlier than anticipated – and needed to be paid for on receipt – Greg was expected to provide these initial funds.

Greg was a little taken aback to think that Tom had both ordered stock without consultation and expected him to provide the financial backing for their business. The speed with which their business dealings had progressed was also of concern to him. He reassured himself that their friendship went back a long way – though he also inwardly squirmed to remember that he hadn't 'felt right' about Tom even during their school years. Occasionally, Greg began to get waves of nausea or a sense of rising panic, both of which he subdued with medication. He'd also resorted to using medication to sleep, and was habitually drinking two stiff scotches at night instead of his occasional one. Again, he dismissed his stress as understandable.

The saga continued and went from bad to worse, as did Greg's sleeping patterns. He increased the medication he was taking to gain some sleep. The psoriasis he'd had under control since his early twenties flared up significantly. His alcohol consumption increased further and he sacrificed his usual recreational activities for time spent working on this new venture.

When the products ordered by Tom arrived, they were of poor quality and the competition in the marketplace was already well established. Tom disappeared interstate, leaving Greg and his wife to pick up the very expensive pieces. Greg felt his reputation was on the line and that he'd have to make good the sticky mess Tom had got him into.

This put Greg and Helen under enormous financial pressure. They had to cancel a long-anticipated overseas trip and sell some properties to meet the shortfall. One of the properties they had to sell had been a gift from Helen's father for her twenty-first birthday. Its income had always provided her with 'pocket money' and although she had readily agreed to its sale, Greg felt mortified that he should have let her (and her father) down so badly. Greg saw his plans for any retirement – let alone an early one – evaporating.

But the turmoil this situation was creating within Greg was far worse than the more obvious outer ramifications of his financial problems. He became moody and depressed and was consumed by disappointment, bitterness and anger. Most of his feelings were directed not at Tom but at himself. How could he have let himself be duped in this way? Why didn't he follow his established business practices? What stopped him from speaking up at crucial moments? Why had he been so trusting? He felt embarrassed, no, *mortified*, by his own stupidity. His inner antenna had given him plenty of cause for alarm yet he had done nothing. How could he have let himself be swayed by someone like Tom?

Greg found the answers to some of these questions very distasteful. He felt vulnerable as his confidence and faith in himself disappeared. He fluctuated between being angry – which at least felt powerful – and ashamed that he'd let himself down so badly. He likewise felt deep shame for creating so much stress and upset for Helen.

Integrity and honesty had always been the hallmarks of his business dealings, and these feelings of shame only precipitated more questions about Greg's self-worth. His belief that if he conducted his life with honesty and integrity nothing untoward would ever happen to him was shattered.

Greg felt himself sliding down into the abyss of helplessness and unexpressed rage he'd dragged himself out of in his youth. In his worst moments he felt he'd accomplished nothing since his teens and that his father's desertion of him was completely justified. At these times, he felt responsible for his parents' marriage break-up and the awful pain he'd seen his mother endure when his father left, and then the ultimate desertion – when he died. Some days he said he felt like a silly, worthless kid again. His father's words echoed in his ears – you'll never amount to anything unless you live honestly and work hard – and only made his stomach churn more with anguish and shame.

Now, 18 months later, he was a shadow of his former self – not only because of the effects of bowel cancer, but because of self-judgement and the inability to forgive himself.

The diagnosis of cancer and its threat to his life and love of Helen provided the impetus for Greg to find healing around this event. At first he felt that everything else had gone wrong so why shouldn't he also get cancer – after all, he deserved it. But as the anguish and implications of this thinking increased, Greg ached to find another way of seeing his situation. As Michelangelo said, 'Only when I began to prepare myself for death, did I but realise that I was learning to live.'

If Greg was going to die, he wanted to find peace first. As he talked, it became obvious that self-forgiveness was his major task – a task precipitated by this recent event but which really stemmed from the more distant occurrences of his youth. He felt he needed to forgive himself for what he'd seen as greed – a quality he loathed in others. Greg saw the opportunity to make some quick money and had overlooked his business practices in his haste and enthusiasm borne of greed. He could also see that his motive of wanting an earlier retirement so that he could spend time with Helen doing the things they loved was fairly innocent and an understandable human desire.

We tend to loathe in others what we often decline to notice in ourselves! On probing, Greg believed his father had been greedy –

after all, they'd had a family life that seemed fine to Greg until his father wanted more. Until our conversation, he'd never seen it as greed. Greg had rationalised in his own mind that it was because of him, rather than his beloved mother, that his father had left for greener pastures. Greg's father was killed in an accident six months after he'd left his family and that had only reinforced that he, Greg, would never let his desire for more form the basis of a decision.

These realisations provided Greg with opportunities to see things differently. In the space of an hour the shackles of guilt, shame, judgement, bitterness and self-blame dissolved with the tears. Greg revisited the events of his youth with more compassion for both himself and his father. He understood that everyone had been doing the best they knew how, given who they were at the time, and what they had made of their history. This compassion enabled Greg to embrace the vulnerable aspects of himself and to recommit to his own life and healing. To find peace we must sometimes venture through the heart of pain. As Goethe says, 'The quickest way out is through.'

Paradoxically, those who embrace their life and healing in this way often experience prolonged or unexpected remissions, unforeseen improvements in health or wellbeing, or a reduction in pain and other symptoms. Any doctor who believes that stress plays no role in the advent of cancer has never stopped to hear their patients' stories!

Peace is a powerful healer. It's not really surprising when we realise that we literally change our biology when we transform the feelings we experience. Allowing the chemicals of shame, self-doubt, despair, anxiety, panic, rage, fear, self-loathing, frustration, resentment or anger to circulate in our body without resolution is no way to build health. The feelings in themselves are not the problem. It is the unwillingness or inability to release them that causes the problem. Forgiveness is the foundation of healing.

By consciously choosing to witness or express our feelings,

rather than unconsciously reacting to them or suppressing them, we release ourselves from their influence.

We need the flexibility and resilience of a tree as we move through the encounters of our lives. A tree yields to the elements, weathering the storm without losing its groundedness in mother Earth from whom it draws its strength, nourishment and refreshment.

Likewise through the practice of awareness borne of meditation, we develop a deep connection with our own source, our essence, so that we weather the events of our life and do not take them so personally. They are not personal vendettas against us; what matters is our response to these events. It is this that makes our experience a positive or negative one.

Liberation from Patterns

The process by which we generally liberate ourselves from the patterns that keep us bound to the past begins when we see ourselves habitually reacting to events or people and decide we want to change to a more appropriate response. This is the 'That's it! Enough! Something's got to change and it's me' phase. We recognise that the patterns of habitual reactions only bring us repeated suffering and we're over it.

The realisation that these habitual patterns permeate all aspects of our life can be disconcerting. Take heart, there may be only two or three fundamental core beliefs that are our challenge to relinquish! A couple of mine, for instance, have been, 'I don't deserve to exist' – which I adopted as a very young child in reaction to my brother Brenden's dominating presence – and 'I'll never be enough' – for similar reasons. Regardless of the number, however, such patterns influence so many aspects of our existence: our choice of friends or partner, career (whether we attempt work or not), suburb, house or car, the food we eat, the environments we frequent, the clothing we wear, how and with whom we sleep, what we do in our recreation time, as well as how we approach situations, and so on.

Realising how these patterns affect us can be quite confusing and upsetting as we see the web – *of our own construction* – that we're caught in. Life didn't inflict these patterns on us. It just *was* that way and our reactions are our own. It's not about whose fault it was or is. It's not about wrong or right or what should have happened. It just happened the way it happened.

When we take responsibility for our peace we understand that we are the cause of whatever we think or feel – no-one makes us think or feel anything. There are aspects of our awakening to this reality that are solitary by nature; when we recognise that the ultimate responsibility for our quality of life lies with us. This leads us to a deep understanding of our very existence. Unless we have that, we cannot make peace with ourselves, with others or with life itself.

This doesn't mean that we have consciously created our suffering. But bringing our unconscious reactions to awareness so that we can examine them and their effects provides the opportunity to see the cause of our suffering so that we can choose differently. Everything that happens to us, then, can be perceived as an opportunity for us to awaken and choose differently. It is easy to forget this and feel that we are victims of what happens, which of course, demands nothing from us and means we remain locked in blaming the world for our unhappiness.

I do not mean to make insignificant some of the appalling things that have happened to people. I have heard stories from people who have been tortured, blown up, raped under terrifying duress, victimised, set alight, bashed, stalked and more. I have listened to parents whose children have been murdered, abused, kidnapped or raped, or who have disappeared or died unexpectedly through accident or illness. No-one asks for these events to happen. When they do happen, we cannot immediately move to a place of acceptance, forgiveness and peace. If we *are* to have peace and healing around such violent physical assaults or tragic losses, then we must first witness or express the accumulated feelings of the traumatic event before we can acknowledge what has happened without being overwhelmed or permanently limited by it. Serious trauma has the potential to literally change the way the brain functions. The chemicals produced by shock mean that habitual re-activation of images can be very difficult to release. This healing takes time and cannot be rushed. It can be facilitated by knowledge and understanding of the emotional healing process. It requires compassion for, and a willingness to embrace, the wounded part of ourselves.

Sometimes, after such traumatic events, our friends and family are keen to see us return unscathed to our former life. They don't necessarily understand that these events fundamentally change us and there is no returning to who we were before. However, we can grow into wiser people who might choose to put in place suitable structures to reassure ourselves and keep us safe in the future. This requires consciously managing the journey rather than feeling a helpless victim of it. It may well be essential and appropriate to identify ways in which we feel we can safely engage with life again after any major trauma.

Some people get stuck in the rage, grief, bitterness or resentment of an event that robbed them of their innocence, confidence or trust in life. Reason and logic have no place in these circumstances and the only appropriate response is compassion. If we do not want to remain defined by the experience then we need to find ways of embracing our inner wounds with compassion. Skilled assistance is often very helpful in this process, particularly when we feel stuck with our fears or feelings and find them unbearably limiting. If any such trauma has occurred in your life, demand that your intuition be present and guide you towards appropriate people who can assist you in creating healing in your life.

If you don't expect personal growth or self-realisation to be an easy path then you won't be disappointed! In my residential and other programs, people often seem to be seeking the rosy path or fast track to healing and peace. They generally don't want to hear about the thorny bits where we need to front up and let go of that which is familiar, even though we know it causes our suffering. Yet, how can we be grateful and respectful of who we are now unless we take on board the journey that brought us to this place? Many people want the simple recipe for peace and don't want to know about the anguish, the tears, the frustration, the challenge and the opportunities that our reactions present us with.

Coming to this process of self-realisation is the *only* reason we're breathing, and is not something we need to get over so that our life can begin. This *is* our life and is the only reason we're here on the planet. We're not here for the kids, the career or the mortgage. We're here to make the moment-by-moment journey of our life *via* the kids, the career, the mortgage. As the saying goes, 'Before enlightenment, chop wood, carry water. After enlightenment, chop wood, carry water.' The outer circumstances of our life may not look different but our view of them shifts dramatically.

This shift in perception liberates us because we understand that we no longer have to react as a child and can choose new responses to life. If we ask ourselves, 'How old do I feel now?' when we catch ourselves in the moment of reaction, the answer often brings tears or feelings of vulnerability and the realisation that we feel like a little kid who's frightened and doesn't know what to do. We need to be gentle with ourselves, and treat each encounter as an opportunity to practise a more appropriate response. We can also ask ourselves, 'Who's in charge right now?' If the answer is our unhealed inner child, we can then find another part of us that can 'parent' that inner child so that we can more easily make an appropriate response rather than continue to simply react.

Once we are aware of our habitual patterns, the path to liberating ourselves from them becomes simple. We have the rest of our lives to liberate ourselves from that which would keep us bound to past re-actions; and to realise how perfect and complete each moment is, as well as our place within it.

By learning to live in harmony with our true self, our inner and outer worlds become congruent and we no longer feel that split reality between who we present to the world and who we are privately to ourselves.

Conscious Thinking

Real thinking is something most of us rarely do. The endless chatter of our mind's reactions to what's going on around us is often what's thought of as thinking. What if real thinking were a conscious process involving the use of our will plus an integrated physical, mental, emotional and spiritual presence?

An effective practice you can use to bring your mind to rest in the present follows. This practice is excellent preparation for conscious thinking. Keep pen and paper handy to jot down thoughts as they form. Read through the passage first then create your own practice and observe your experience.

Practice

Settle yourself in a chair with your feet flat on the floor; let your eyes remain open, keep your spine comfortably erect, let your hands rest on your knees or in your lap. Begin by taking some long, slow, deep breaths, perhaps breathing in through your nose and out through your mouth in a long sigh. Breathing in relaxation, breathing out all activity in the mind, in the body. Gently in, gently out. Continue breathing deeply until you feel yourself physically relax.

Bring your awareness into the present moment by connecting with the senses of your body. Be aware of your surroundings. Feel your weight and posture. Be aware of the pressure of the chair, your clothing. Notice textures, pressure and temperature, releasing any tension. Feel the air against your cheeks and hands. Be aware of all the sounds around you, within and outside the space you're in. Not judging, not resisting. Just listening into the stillness from which all sound arises. Let your listening expand until you hear your heartbeat or the clouds passing by.

Enjoy the breath. Breathing in. Rest. Breathing out. Rest. Breathing in, rest, and so on. Feel the quality of the air entering your nostrils. Not thinking about anything, just observing. The body at rest, the mind at rest. Simply being, absorbed in this present moment, full of life's unfolding.

If the mind becomes distracted, bring it back to the practice of breathing in, breathing out. Silently, in your mind, you could continue repeating the words 'Breathing in, breathing out' with each inward and outward breath respectively.

A sense of being fully conscious, wide awake and deeply relaxed, open to each sound, sensation, feeling, thought – holding onto nothing. Letting each sound, sensation, feeling or thought, come to pass.

When the mind becomes still, focus on the subject of your interest.

Your intention is to explore more deeply your understanding of the issue.

Your responsibility – response-ability – is to remain in the present and observe the mind range over various aspects of the subject. We remain in the present by maintaining our awareness of our senses.

Throughout this process our awareness ranges over the full spectrum of our being. We note physical reactions. What was it that caused us to react by tensing or releasing, cringing from or opening to? Not trying to work it out. Simply observing. Notice if and what your mind dismisses, hesitates over, emphasises, refuses to allow. Simply witnessing without judgement, without mental chatter. Letting the ideas arise and formulate. Allowing new relationships and connections between previously isolated ideas to form.

End of practice section.

There is a joy and satisfaction in this process. It has a fulfilling sense of *using* our mind, instead of being used *by* our mind.

Watching ideas come into being, silently witnessing the creation of new concepts, understandings, new connections, revelations. It's a little like clicking on 'Find' in the computer. We simply need to witness what the mind presents in response to our desire to think about something.

Our inner antenna and intuition will bring all relevant information to our attention or give us the nudge we need to seek further information so that it can be incorporated. With practice, thinking becomes a pleasure. It's very different to the constant chatter we're so often absorbed by. With the regular practice of meditation, which is discussed in detail in the following chapter, the constant background chatter of the mind completely stops and the way the brain and mind functions actually changes. It is an invaluable tool in the process of waking up and being profoundly present to life's unfolding potential. If we don't wake up we're destined to relive our history.

The Power of Language

It is very helpful to become aware of our language and the way we express ourselves. There are words we often use that keep us habitually bound to the past. Becoming conscious of what these are and when we use them, and changing them – even in mid-sentence – can become our practice until such diligence is no longer required.

In order to have this choice, we need to be present and aware of what we habitually say when we feel the victim of our circumstance. The words we use when we feel this way limit our potential. These limiting words might include statements that begin with 'I can't . . .', 'I should . . .', 'I have to . . .', 'I never . . .', 'I always . . .'.

These words (and what follows them) are the language of the victim. By becoming aware of our language we can release ourselves from feeling like the helpless victim of our history. A full list of the words that formulate the language of the victim appears towards the end of this chapter.

Look at the following sentence: 'I can't deal with spiders.' What we're really saying is that 'We won't deal with spiders' because the fact is we almost certainly *can* deal with spiders. It is because we willingly give our power to the long-held *fear* of spiders that we're dominated by our inability to respond. Our power going to the fear is the reaction we want to heal so that a *response* becomes our choice. We can then change the sentence to,

'I choose not to deal with spiders because I respect the fear I hold.' This is closer to the truth if we want to be an active participator rather than a helpless victim. Or we could say, 'Up until now I haven't been able to deal with spiders, however today I'm going to deal with this one.'

Here's another example: 'I can't speak before an audience' may become 'I choose not to speak before an audience' or 'I have decided to learn the skills of speaking before an audience' or 'I will speak before an audience.' These three latter ways of expressing ourselves feel far more powerful than saying, 'I can't . . .'. In the now, the present, it becomes our conscious choice rather than our unconscious reaction.

Next, we become aware of the words in mid-sentence and we may or may not stop them. We see the consequences of speaking them more clearly and mutter to ourselves, 'I *did* it [said it] again!' This is excellent progress, as we are becoming more aware of the potential to change.

Then we hear ourselves in mid-sentence and choose to change the words. For example, we might change 'I can't deal with spiders' to 'I've decided (not) to deal with this spider'; or 'I can't speak in public' to 'Thank you for asking me, however I choose not to speak in public' or 'Thank you for asking me, I'd be delighted to speak' and then consider what you'll need to do to prepare yourself for the event!

Public speaking can be an extremely stressful undertaking and many people are fearful of it. Being passionate about the subject on which we're to speak certainly helps, because then we can speak from the heart, which is really saying we can speak our truth.

When I was first asked to speak publicly it was a considerable ordeal for me. So considerable that my hand shook uncontrollably, I spilled water down the front of my jacket, felt the onset of a panic attack, and excused myself and sat down within two minutes of what was meant to be a 20-minute talk feeling like a wet fool!

When I had leukaemia, however, I decided that I didn't want to go to my grave as full of fear as I had been for the first 33 years of my life. I vowed that when fear appeared, I'd embrace it and work with it until it was no more. Since that first disastrous encounter with an audience, I've given countless talks, speeches and interviews in an array of settings from community halls to Parliament House, international conferences and on radio and television. I choose to not let fear dominate my life. I am not saying that any of this is easy. What I *am* saying is: what else is there to do between now and death but liberate ourselves from the fears that would keep us bound?

After choosing to change our victim language mid-sentence, we next become aware of a habitual thought or reaction in our mind and choose not to utter it. Of course we fluctuate between these stages for a time, depending upon the heat or excitement of the moment and the level of our awareness in it! We must be gentle and compassionate with ourselves as our mind struggles with the unfamiliar.

Finally, we come to the point where the thought or reaction doesn't even enter our mind because the ramifications are so obvious that we wouldn't choose (in a million years) to go back to simply reacting to life. Once the lid is off the Pandora's box and we're destined for the return journey to a truer representation of our self, there is no turning back. There may be plateaus, there may be dead-ends as our mind struggles to maintain its embedded fears, beliefs, justifications, reactions and defences, but the outcome is certain.

Beware of justifications or defensiveness. For instance, you may have habitually said 'Yes' to people in the past when your whole inner being shrieked 'No!'. Yes, I'll be there; yes, I'll do that; yes, I'll come. And probably unconsciously resenting the fact that you've been at everyone's beck and call. If we want peace of mind, we must be willing to release ourselves from resentment so that our inner and outer worlds become congruent. In this way our life becomes more authentic.

Managing Time

What is predictable about time is that you can never catch up to it. The future always lies ahead of you and the past is always behind you. No matter how much effort you put into trying to do so, you cannot bring either the future or the past into the present.

We've all heard the expression, 'time is of the essence'. Put another way, we want time *now* to be spent in ways that support and nourish our essence – our sacred inner self.

No matter how many time-saving devices we invent, ample time still seems to elude us. Many people complain that there simply isn't enough time in the day for them to accomplish everything either at work or in their leisure, let alone to have some time for themselves. We sometimes talk about time as if it had elastic sides, as if we can cram in more and more things until we run out of it.

There are 168 hours in every week and every one of them is ours. I've checked it out internationally and found it's the same everywhere. It doesn't matter what country we're in, what language we speak, what position we hold, whether we're male or female – everyone gets 168 hours each week to spend *as they choose*.

Although that's probably not what a majority of us feel. We may feel that other people or situations demand our time and we might be resenting some of the hours we spend doing the things we feel were not our choice. We may be at a time in our life where we want to review how we're spending our time. The following story, a composite of many, illustrates this well.

Jane's father, Edward, lived in a nursing home an hour from her home. Alzheimer's had stripped away the vestiges of his personality, leaving him distant, confused and unable to recognise anything or anyone. Jane, a single mum, held a job in the city as a solicitor and life revolved around her work, her three boys, her home and the weekly visits to her father on weekends.

Her mother, Phyllis, had died two years earlier and Jane felt duty-bound to continue the visits to her father that her mother had established before her fatal heart attack. Jane took on the purchasing and laundering of her father's pyjamas as her mother had always done. Edward had always been particular about his pyjamas and insisted on red flannelette ones. Laundering them herself, just as her mother had done, became her only option, as otherwise they'd get circulated amongst all of the inmates of the nursing home and there'd be no guarantee he'd see them again after the first wearing. She'd spent frustrating hours on the phone calling local and sometimes distant shops to locate red flannelette pyjamas, and then had driven kilometres out of her way to purchase them.

Jane and her mother had always been close friends and shared an easy intimacy that Jane still grieved for. She missed being able to pick up the phone to talk about her achievements, disappointments, the problems with her children – now teenagers – or her pangs of loneliness as a meaningful relationship seemed so remote. Sometimes she'd caught herself ringing her mother's number before the numbing pain of missing her would return with the realisation of her absence. Their conversations were by no means one-sided, as Phyllis had shared some of the challenges she'd experienced living with Jane's father. At first Phyllis had talked reluctantly, feeling she was being disloyal to Edward, but over the years there was an easy understanding between mother and daughter about the difficulties Phyllis had endured.

After he'd returned from the war, Edward, like many men, had devoted himself to creating and building a business. His education had been interrupted by the war and, as he achieved financial success, he'd often claimed over the years that he was a self-made man. Though she'd frequently heard her father say that he'd worked long and hard only for his family, she had regrets about his absence when she was a child growing up, and had felt slightly in awe, perhaps even afraid of him. Much of his business kept him away from home and there were times she'd woken late at night to hear arguments between her parents. She would huddle under the covers and sometimes cry herself back to sleep. Alcohol played an increasing role in both the arguments and his absences. His drinking had increased with the failure of one of his businesses and Jane found that she could not remember some of her childhood years. She'd left home for university with relief, and threw herself into her law studies.

As a young woman, Jane had questioned Phyllis over her decision to stay with her father. Phyllis seemed resigned to her fate and would sometimes even defend Edward's actions – he'd been through the war, he provided a home and lifestyle she enjoyed, and she felt that he was basically a good man. Jane understood her mother well as she too had ambivalent feelings for him. Edward had provided her with a comfortable upbringing where she lacked for nothing, including the funds for her school and then university education. He'd been a grandparent of sorts to her children and he'd given her sage counsel on many occasions. Edward had always carried himself with an air of confidence and strength, and she'd found both comfort and fear in that, depending on the circumstances.

However, now that he was beyond all response, the weekly visits to her father began to take on a feeling of dread. She'd arrive at the nursing home with an armful of clean red pyjamas and a heavy heart. Jane found the smell of him and the place, and her father's stubbly chin, scaly skin and unblinking stare almost unbearable. She was feeling increasingly resentful and angry about his behaviour in the past. The mere thought of Saturday and its routine obligatory visits tainted her leisure moments, such as they were, grabbed after her responsibilities for the day were complete.

It saddened her too to realise that most of her interactions with her sons seemed a litany of behaviour corrections. She'd long stopped rejoicing with warmth and love in their innocence and spirited beings. This added to her guilt because her sons didn't readily choose her company and she'd had to admit to herself that she was no fun to be with. She saw *that* as the reason no man wanted to have a relationship with her either. Jane felt she should be able to cope better than she was, and likewise used that judgement against herself.

Loaded into her resentment about her visits to her father was the fact that she didn't feel she had a life of her own. Indeed, she felt that her whole life had become obligatory. The resentment Jane felt and the feelings of entrapment finally consumed most of her waking hours until it all came to a point of crisis.

One Saturday afternoon she'd dropped off her boys at soccer and was driving to visit her father when she had a minor accident involving another car and found herself sobbing helplessly at the wheel. It was in this moment that Jane reached the, 'That's it! I'm over doing it this way. Something's got to change' state that I wrote of earlier.

This incident provided sufficient impetus for Jane to seek help, as she was no longer willing to allow her life to be consumed by the perceived demands of others.

The accident was the 'last straw' that became the catalyst for change. Jane recognised that even though she *outwardly* appeared to be coping with the demands in her life, she was *inwardly* in turmoil, feeling anxious, irritated, 'put upon', resentful and unhappy. These feelings of being overwhelmed by her life impinged on her ability to concentrate, her capacity for humour, joy and spontaneity, her ability to be present to her children and to her own needs. Her confidence in her own perceptions was also threatened as she put everyone else's needs before her own. We have only to consider Jane's story to see the moment-by-moment contribution that bottled-up feelings can have on our physical health.

I am convinced that this chemical wash flowing moment by precious moment throughout our bodies, in addition to environmental pollutants, what we eat and how we live, activates – or doesn't activate – our genetic predispositions. We may have the genetic predisposition for a whole range of possibilities that only become active when exposed to this chemical state of consciousness. It is in the minutiae of life that we're significantly contributing to our physical health.

We feel trapped and sapped until we reach the point that Jane did. It's not that the feelings are the problem, as all the feelings Jane experienced are understandable. The problem lies in bottling them up without the capacity to either witness and transform them or give them healthy expression. Indeed, Jane judged herself harshly for feeling the way she did and expected herself to cope better.

If we want peace *more than anything* then we need to devote time to our own healing. It needs to be our priority.

We've so often been told that to focus on ourselves is selfish. Yet, when we consider this more deeply, we realise that the greatest gift we can give ourselves, our children, our family, community or the planet, is the gift of our own good physical, mental, emotional and spiritual health – indeed, then we might be useful for something. If we don't take responsibility for the creation of our own health on all levels, chances are someone else will end up having to do so.

Our children learn most effectively not from what we say but from what they see us do. We can be a living demonstration to them of what it is to live life skilfully. This means a spiritually based life, lived from the inside out. Children are aching for this information. Yet there are very few resources to provide guidance on how to conduct the journey of their lives in this challenging world in a way that is deeply meaningful.

I have heard Jane's story told in a thousand ways by people who've come for counselling or attended Quest for Life Centre programs.

These people are often productive, capable and skilled in their lives yet lack deep contentment and feel that something is missing. The characters and events may differ in our stories, yet in each one there comes a time when we each want to own our life and live it in a way that we find deeply satisfying and meaningful. The unattended wounds of the past and our efforts to minimise their influence in the present and future all have consequences.

Living with inner authority over how we spend our time can be challenging to cultivate yet it is the foundation of our growth in consciousness. We will not grow if we do not take responsibility for our own life. We will not grow if we're preoccupied with what others are doing. We will not grow waiting for others to change. We will not grow for as long as our focus is on changing the world. We will not grow if we stay stuck in our reactions from the patterns of the past.

The crisis is in our consciousness, not in the world.

J Krishnamurti

The moment-by-moment effect on our health of perpetuating self-defeating behaviours and negative or limiting self-talk is what ails us. Our physical health is simply a consequence.

Like Jane, you might now decide to weigh up how you *choose* to spend your time more consciously.

For instance, if someone asks you to do something, instead of reacting with a 'Yes' that you later regret, you can respond with, 'Thank you for asking me. I will check my diary and call you.' And until you're familiar with owning your own time, don't reach for your diary! This gives you the opportunity to consider whether what is on offer is congruent with how you now *choose* to spend your time.

Another excellent response to something you already know you no longer want to do is, 'Thank you for asking me but I'm fully committed at present.' This statement is impossible to argue with and requires no justification!

This inner work has consequence. For instance, if you want peace of mind more than anything, you might want to consider whether gossipy energy is useful to you now. We know that gossip is a way of feeding on other people's stories and it never leads to upliftment, empowerment or inspiration. We may realise that some (even all!) of our friends and acquaintances or family gossip, and if we're to sacrifice such relationships where will that leave us? Sometimes we need to let go of people in our life before new, more rewarding relationships can develop.

If we want to respond to the events and encounters in our life rather than react to them, consider the following chart of 'I' statements from both the perspective of the victim and the active participant.

The language of the victim contains words borne of our reactions. The active participant uses words that embody our ability to respond, rather than react.

VICTIM	ACTIVE PARTICIPANT
I can't . . .	*I won't . . .*
	I choose (not) to . . .
	I don't want to . . .
	I've decided (not) to . . .
I have to . . .	*I will . . .*
I should . . .	*I want to . . .*
I must . . .	*I've decided to . . .*
I ought to . . .	*I choose (not) to . . .*
I don't have time . . .	*I've decided to do something else.*
	That's not my priority right now.

We can train ourselves to be keenly aware when these victim words
and the words listed below come out of our mouths. These words
are the vocabulary we use when we are operating from the habitual patterns of the past. Once you have become aware of them, they
won't leave your lips so easily. Sometimes the whole sentence
escapes and we again see the limiting consequences of that pattern.
Or we can catch the words as they are coming out of our mouths
and choose to change the statement to one that has us as the participant rather than the victim. Then we see the words come into
our mind and we choose not to let them come out of our mouths.
We fluctuate between these three states – seeing the consequences
after we have uttered the words; catching ourselves in mid-sentence
and changing them; and being aware of the words and choosing
not to utter them – for some time before they no longer even come
into our mind.

Other words that you'll benefit from either omitting from your
vocabulary or only using with keen awareness, include:

Try: Either commit to it or don't, after all, who's in
                     charge of your time now? To say, 'I'll try and be
                     there on Saturday' leaves the door open to a better
                     offer or implies that your schedule is not in your
                     control. 'I'm trying to lose weight': you've either
                     committed to losing weight or not. Again, who's in
                     charge? 'I'll try and work harder': is it realistic and
                     appropriate and, if so, what stops us from simply
                     committing to making a more appropriate effort?
                     There is no need for the word 'try' in our vocabu-
                     lary – unless we're playing rugby!

If only . . .:   We generally use 'if only' when we're resisting
                     what is.
                          'If only she'd left five minutes later', 'If only

you'd listen to me', 'If only I was as smart as my brother', 'If only it wasn't raining', 'If only I was slimmer', and so on. We need to accept what is and make the transition to respond to the situation in which we find ourselves. The word, 'if' can be problematic on its own sometimes, too. We can spend a good deal of time and energy hypothesising over what might happen, what could happen and probably won't happen. Again, be aware of its presence in your vocabulary.

Impossible: Very few things are impossible, though it certainly takes longer to achieve what we perceive as impossible.

Never/always: These words often sneak into reactive conversations. 'You never listen to me', 'I always thought you'd amount to nothing', 'You never put the rubbish out', 'You always leave your clothes on the floor', 'You're always grumpy'. These are sweeping generalisations and their intent is often to wound the other person, or ourselves. It is better to use these words with great awareness. As Janine Shepherd titled her book about her remarkable recovery from a very serious bicycle accident: *Never Tell Me Never*.

But: Have you ever had a conversation where the other person says, 'I agree with everything you've said, but . . .' then they list all the reasons why they disagree with your argument? There are certainly uses for 'but' but I'd suggest you be aware when using it! We can sometimes use the word 'and' instead of 'but'. For instance, in the previous statement we could instead say, 'I agree with everything you've said and I'm wondering how that might affect xyz . . .'. In this way we might build upon one another's ideas instead of seeing them in an adversarial way.

This is not a definitive list but it is a good start to becoming more aware of the language we use. You will see that when you begin to put some of these ideas into practice, they actually shift your perspective from the world outside of yourself to the world within – your own consciousness.

When we live our lives from the point of our essence – from the inside out – we can experience equanimity, open-heartedness and joy even in the midst of pain and suffering. We each have our own unique set of beliefs based on our history and what we've made of it. Some of these beliefs are particular to us as an individual; our family, culture or nation will share others. We've all picked up beliefs and attitudes about life, relationships and the world from our earliest childhood memories. We view the world through these accumulated beliefs and make judgements about others and ourselves in accordance with the beliefs we hold.

What do we do in our lives when we're confronted with a personal situation that we simply can't fix, change or make better? Say we've just heard a friend's child has been killed in an accident. Some people disappear and can't be seen for dust. They've glanced the outer mirror of their worst nightmare and they bolt in reaction. They don't know what to say, what to do or how to be in the presence of anguish and will cross the street or duck for cover if they see their friend, the child's parent, coming.

Other people barricade their hearts behind inane comments which are meant to ease suffering but only increase its intensity. These folk may say things like, 'She's in God's care now' or 'Be strong. Heaven or God needed her more than you' or 'Take comfort. You've got your other children to love' or 'You can always have another child', or some other trite comment.

That's why my favourite bumper sticker continues to be 'My karma just ran over your dogma' – so often people try to make sense of suffering when reason is not what's called for. Compassion is called for, not reason. It's better to say, 'I can't imagine how you're feeling right now but I'm here' or better still, 'I'm here with a casserole for dinner and I've got time if you want to talk.'

In order to accompany one another into the caverns of hell – our worst nightmare – and keep our hearts wide open, we will benefit from a strong connection to that which is unchangeable – our essence or spirit. In this way, our hearts expand in compassion to embrace the pain and anguish and are not diminished by them.

Kate was nine years old when I met her. She had cancer of the heart muscle that ended her life when she was just ten. On one of her visits to me she had drawn a picture of Garfield the cat. In the bubble of his thoughts were three coloured hearts. Kate told me that she'd drawn me two pictures but she'd put them on her windowsill and the wind had blown the other picture away. I asked her what was in the other picture. She said, 'It was exactly the same as this one but the hearts were all shattered down the middle.' I said to her, 'Perhaps the wind was telling you that you don't need to have broken hearts.' Kate replied as if being patient with a young child, 'No Petrea, you don't understand. Sometimes hearts have to break before they heal.' She told me she'd draw me another picture to replace the one that blew away, which she did. Her pictures appear in my book about grief and loss which Kate also titled: *Sometimes Hearts Have to Break*.

It was Kate, very early on in my practice, who gave me the courage to let my own heart break over and over as people told me the sad stories of their lives, or as I witnessed their self-loathing or judgement. My experience is that when we allow our hearts to break, they heal, and indeed grow bigger because of the scar tissue. In this way we create enough heart to contain the anguish and still have the capacity to love; the anguish does not diminish or belittle our capacity to love and we don't give our power to embitterment.

We resist letting our hearts break because it hurts and we want the hurting to stop. However, these are growing pains that we need not resist. As our heart expands without resistance or judgement to embrace the pain, anguish and suffering of others and ourselves, we offer a loving space in which can be uttered what has been unspeakable up until then. And in the giving of that gift we abundantly receive the treasures of another person's truth. In this instance giving and receiving are perceived as the same thing. Such is the gift we can be to one another. We become one another's saviour.

Do not wait for another teacher or saviour to come. Organised religions, cliques, cults and all exclusive groupings ask individual members to give their allegiance to an idea and / or personality outside themselves. Giving anyone permission to make decisions for you robs you of your own creative freedom. We have had the teachings delivered to us over and over through the Buddha, Jesus, Krishna, Mohammed, Yogananda, St Francis, *A Course in Miracles* and countless other people and books. It is time for each of us to put into daily practice what we know. Live the teachings now and be the teacher to others in your life.

Awareness and the constant practice of non-attachment to thoughts, judgements, beliefs and feelings leads to that which is beyond the vagaries of change. Through the deep silence of meditation we return again and again to replenish and refresh ourselves from this inner wellspring of compassion, wisdom and joy – our essence – until we need return no more, this source becoming our home and refuge, our beginning and ending place.

A good day of worrying is far more exhausting than a good day with an axe. The energy squandered by a mind consumed by the future and the past is considerable and leaves us weary at day's end. Practising self-awareness is the key to having choice in our lives and to liberating ourselves from unconscious mental activity.

One of the greatest gifts we can give our body and mind is the gift of meditation. The profound sense of ease and peace brings healing and awareness to our life. We cannot see the patterns and beliefs that play out in our lives without awareness. We are destined to unconsciously react from these patterns until light dawns and we realise that it's not a matter of changing the world but changing our perceptions of the world.

Meditation becomes that sacred space in which we replenish and refresh ourselves and experience the profound connection with our own consciousness. When we quieten the internal chatter of our minds, we discover the place from which intuition, joy, inspiration, imagination, wisdom, contentment and more effort-lessly flow.

CHAPTER 6

Meditation Matters

Nothing has to be achieved in order to be at peace.
All we have to do is stop doing – stop wanting
things to be different, stop worrying, stop getting
upset when things don't go as we would wish, or
when people don't behave as we think they should.
When we stop doing all the things
that obscure the peace that is there at our core,
we find that what we have been seeking all along is
there, waiting silently for us.

Peter Russell

Meditation enables us to be more skilful at living in
the present.

Me

You are the landscape and not the storm.

James Thornton

Understanding often requires a retreat into stillness,
a movement away from frustration toward an
expectant listening,
an openness to understanding paired
with a willingness to go without understanding
until you have become ready to receive it.

Rachel Naomi Remen

Meditation has no particular religious connection though the mystics of every great religion practise it in some form. Meditation creates the rich possibility of experiencing all that is sacred within and around us. It's the state in which we directly experience our true nature, our essence, our consciousness, our connection to the creative spirit.

It is quite likely that we have all experienced meditation without being aware that it was called that. We might have many such memories or we might have to dig deep, perhaps back to childhood, to remember the luminous moments when the mind was bypassed and beauty, joy, love, a sense of union with all things or a profound moment of peace and realisation struck us. These glimpses of a more fully alive state of awareness stir us in our depths. We yearn for the experience of being rapturously alive. We can all actively work towards living in that conscious awareness.

Meditation becomes a way of life, not just a formal practice one or more times a day. We can live each moment of our lives consciously aware of all that surrounds us and is within us. From this serene state, we respond open-heartedly, moment by moment, to life's encounters. This is living in heaven.

This might sound far-fetched but it's not only possible, it is our ultimate destiny. After all, what is the choice? Would we choose a life laid waste by fear and uncertainty? Life can change in a moment. Our perception of life can likewise change.

We don't meditate to become fabulous meditators. We meditate so that we are more easily able to liberate ourselves from the judgements, attitudes, beliefs, thoughts and patterns which would keep us bound to the past, and to help us to become more skilful at living in the present.

Regular meditation enables us to live with more clarity and choice. It is simple to practise and it establishes a foundation from which we can create our life.

Much of our life is spent taking on more information, more

identities and more learning. We so often identify who we are by what we do – I am an old person, a young person, a mother or father, a teacher, a manager, a plumber, a technician, a truck driver, a carer, a doctor, a massage therapist – believing that our value lies in these accumulations of 'doing' rather than simply in our 'being'. In meditation we find our human 'being' beyond our human 'doings'.

Human endeavour and achievement is often brought about through struggle, strain and tension, whereas in meditation we relax into a deeper sense of ourselves. Meditation is the process of unlearning, of letting go of these false identities – the information we've accumulated about ourselves.

The regular practice of meditation gives us greater presence of mind. With presence of mind comes the possibility of choice: we can continue to *react* to the events of our lives from our unprocessed emotional history or make a more appropriate *response*. Until we are present, aware, awake, we don't see the choice. It is liberating when we react less to events in our life and have a greater ability to respond to them instead.

Note the words, 'presence of mind'. This describes that state of being when the mind is present to what 'is' rather than caught up in the inner world of idle mental chatter. We are not our mind. We are more than a mind. Our responsibility is to quieten the mind so that we can hear the voice of our intuition. Otherwise the mind is forever jumping seconds, minutes, weeks, months or years into the future or into the past. In this way it seeks fulfilment in all the wrong places.

Meditation liberates us from these thoughts and feelings as we develop our ability to witness and release them, but not react *from* them. In this way, we choose new and more appropriate responses to life situations.

While your mind is often absorbed in the future or in the past, your body is always in the present. One of the most effective ways of bringing your mind to rest is to focus on the senses of your body. Do this simple practice now while you're reading these words.

Take a couple of long, slow, deep breaths. As you exhale, feel your body soften and relax. Become aware of your weight and posture. Feel the pressure of the chair against your body, the floor against your feet or whatever your body might be in contact with. Become aware of the space between your feet and the floor. Feel the touch of your clothing against your skin. Notice its texture and the temperature your clothing helps create. Feel the touch of the air against your hands, your cheeks. Become aware of all the sounds within and outside the space you're in – not judging, labelling or resisting anything, simply allowing every sound to be heard, to come to pass. Let your listening travel right out until you hear the silence beyond all sound. This state, where the mind is at rest, is what we're aiming to achieve by focusing it in the present moment.

The more present we are in our own lives, embracing each moment without judgement, the more alive we become. Connecting with the senses of the body can become our constant practice. The mind is forever projecting into the world of what 'isn't' by projecting into the future, which hasn't happened yet, or rehashing, resenting or reliving the past which we cannot change, while our body is immersed in the world of what 'is'.

Meditation gives us greater access to our intuition, which is available to everyone who brings the mind to rest. Intuition only functions when the mind is quiet. The chemical and electrical state of the brain when the mind is quiet makes it available and receptive to information from within and around itself. The chemical and electrical state of the brain when the mind is agitated makes it impossible for our intuition to function.

In time, meditation enables us to live by our intuition. Then we know effortlessly what to do, how to be, where to go, when to speak, when to reach out and touch, when not to, when to stay silent, when to use humour, when to stay with the anguish and say nothing, and so on. Intuition is our greatest guide for living well on the planet. It is the voice of our creative spirit.

In meditation, as the mind quietens and becomes more peaceful, so our body relaxes. Meditation is the state of simply being. It has no religious necessity, though it may be a profoundly spiritual experience. We see the benefits of meditation in our lives through increased clarity, joy, spontaneity, creativity, wisdom, love, confidence, vitality and humour.

Organised groups tend to offer solutions to our spiritual enquiry by insisting we follow a teacher, a guru or master, or a dogmatic teaching. We crave a special teacher, a special teaching and a special experience. A spiritual practice does not necessarily involve a doctrine, a guru or anything imposed from the outside. Your spiritual practice is what you do to be at peace within yourself and in the world. The goal of our spiritual practice is simply to change our perception of ourselves and the world. That becomes our spiritual practice. This practice is the essence of all the world's spiritual traditions.

There are places on the planet and particular people who exude a profound air of peace. This 'air' is a vibrating energy that we may feel as a blessing because it reminds us of something we're seeking within ourselves.

The cave in which I meditated for some months outside of Assisi was just such a place. St Francis used this cave for long periods of prayer and meditation and though that was many hundreds of years ago, there continues to be an atmosphere of tangible bliss within its walls.

It is a tiny cave, which holds not more than half a dozen people at a time. I sat in a corner of the cave for up to 18 hours a day. It also played host to dozens, even hundreds, of visitors on some days. I could hear the advent of their arrival long before they entered the cave.

Some people came reverentially, preparing themselves to soak up its atmosphere. Others came laughing and skipping down the stairs full of chatter and clicking cameras. While I sat, probably unnoticed, with eyes closed in my corner, I would hear the noise subside and notice that people always left in a quieter and more reflective state. In the hours of undisturbed solitude within this cave I found it easier to melt into the bliss that I felt existed within and around me.

Just as there are the chemicals and hormones of stress, so too, our body secretes beneficial chemicals when we experience contentment, peace, joy, love and bliss. When the mind is anxious or stressed, the body secretes many chemicals and hormones into the bloodstream.

Stress itself is not a negative thing. It is essential to have stress in our life. It provides us with grist for the mill, and by embracing challenging stresses we gain satisfaction and fulfilment. However, stress over which we feel we have little or no control can be detrimental to our peace of mind and subsequently to our physical health.

We have a physiological response to stress that, in the right place, is entirely necessary and appropriate. Long ago, when a bear appeared in the mouth of our cave, our body had a distinct physiological response. It pumped powerful hormones and chemicals into our bloodstream that enabled us to either run from the bear or fight it. These hormones and chemicals increased our heart rate and breathing so that oxygenated blood flowed to our muscles, which enabled them to work intensely for our escape or for a fight and gave us a heightened awareness of our immediate circumstances. This mechanism is known as the fight or flight response.

One of the side effects of these chemicals and hormones is that they suppress the immune system. We don't need our immune system when faced with the threat of the bear. We need an increased heartbeat to pump our blood, increased respiration to oxygenate it, and so on. If we're dealing with a physical threat such as a bear, these responses are entirely necessary and appropriate. In running from or fighting the bear we use up all these stress chemicals and hormones, and our body returns to its own natural equilibrium. Then our immune system is again operational and can take care of any cuts, scratches or injuries we might have suffered during our encounter.

Now when we think about our own life, we might feel that our partner is the bear, that our boss is the bear, that an uncertain world is the bear, or that money, time or responsibilities are the bear.

We might have this same physiological response when someone cuts us off in the traffic, when we're involved in an argument, when we're in unfamiliar or fearful situations, when we don't measure up to our own expectations, when we're running late for an appointment. We all, no doubt, are aware of many situations such as these in our life. In these situations we still secrete the same chemicals and hormones but generally have no way of physically using up their effects in our body.

It is inappropriate to physically attack or run away from an erring motorist, partner or antagonist, or from the world or from ourselves. When these chemicals and hormones remain circulating in our body they contribute negatively to our health. It's a little like keeping an engine idling at too high a speed. It defies commonsense to imagine a content and well-functioning immune system – or liver or heart – in the body of someone constantly angry, fearful, bitter, resentful or upset. Likewise if a person feels chronically depressed, helpless, powerless, trapped or hopeless.

Our mind is not separate from our body. Our emotions are not separate from our body. As human beings we're an integrated whole. The beliefs and thoughts that we hold in our mind affect the functioning of our body. The feelings that we have, whether acknowledged or ignored, have an effect on our body. They are our experience of reality and therefore are real for us. Therefore each person's reality is unique to them.

We all have the capacity to change the beliefs that our mind holds dear. This gives us a tremendous point of power in that we can change the beliefs that cause us stress, depression, fear, resentment, hopelessness, powerlessness and frustration into those which lay down the foundations for greater peace, fulfilment and joy in our lives. This choice is unique to humankind.

One of the most powerful tools for change is meditation. There are many techniques of meditation that different people promote. Some believe theirs is the best or the highest! The best technique is the one that works for you. There is no right technique, no higher or lower technique, nor is there one teacher. There are as many techniques and teachers as there are people. Allow yourself the freedom to find the right one for you. The technique is not meditation. It is the tool we use to lead us into the state of meditation.

In meditation the physiological responses to stress, already spoken of, have an opportunity to regain their natural equilibrium. We breathe more slowly, our heart rate and blood pressure drops, our muscles relax, and we come to rest physiologically as the mind begins to settle and a sense of ease is experienced.

Meditation is like relaxation for the mind. It is very simple. Just as we bring our awareness to the various muscles in our body and allow them to soften and relax, so we observe the thoughts and feelings that pass through our mind, through our body. Observe and let go. Not holding on to thoughts or feelings, not adding to them, not resisting them, just observing, and letting go.

Imagine sitting deep beneath the ocean, at rest on the ocean floor. Thoughts are like the waves far above on the surface, they don't disturb our peace. If you find that you're swimming amongst the waves or that you're busy with thoughts, just let them go again. Do the same with feelings that arise; not judging, not criticising yourself for having them, let them come to pass. Observe and let go. An ocean of awareness, not focusing on any particular thought or feeling. Be patient with yourself. Treat meditation like a new adventure into unexplored territory; a journey within yourself.

Avoid falling into the trap of believing that meditation is difficult or requires long practice to become effective. Quite quickly you'll begin to experience the benefits of meditation. You'll notice a calmness in your attitude. The things that used to distress you will become less consequential as you begin to see that everything is unfolding in its own perfect way. Your memory will improve, as will your powers of concentration. You'll also find that you're able to accomplish more in your day and that you have more energy. You may find that you need less sleep and that the sleep you have is deeper and more refreshing. You'll find your sense of humour returning in full force, as will your spontaneity, creativity and confidence in yourself.

Though meditation can be practised in changing circumstances, it can be useful to establish a place of meditation in your home, even if it's in a corner of a room or in a particular chair. After a time you'll find that you relax and become calm as soon as you enter that quiet place – or even thinking of your meditation place will enable you to settle within yourself. If you share your home, you may wish to ask for other people's cooperation during your meditation. Or you might encourage them to join you in your practice.

It doesn't matter if there are sounds around you, though it can be easier to learn in a quiet environment. You may wish to leave a note on the door asking not to be disturbed and to take the telephone off the hook. If you need to break your meditation, you can do so; just take a couple of long, deep breaths, open your eyes and attend to whatever you need to.

Some days meditation comes more easily and the mind settles into silence; most days it requires vigilance and focus! It is easy to say, 'Ah, the one I had in 2003, that was a ripper,' and then compare all subsequent practices to that one! So don't fall into the trap of comparing one meditation practice to another. Let each meditation practice be complete unto itself.

For some of us, when our body relaxes our sense of physicality may disappear. It is common to experience strange physical sensations during meditation practice. These might involve a sense of floating, or that our body seems to have enlarged or disappeared. Some people experience a spinning sensation or nausea. This might be due to low blood pressure or the activation of the subtle energies in the spine, or both. If the cause is low blood pressure (or low haemoglobin, which means a low red blood cell count) then lie down for your practice and return to sitting and being upright very slowly, stretching as you come back to physical activity. Regardless of the physical sensations, continue with the practice of meditation, neither looking for physical signs nor labelling them as they occur.

There may also be a sense of being without a 'personality'. It's as if the 'Petreaness' disappears and we're left with a deep sense of just 'being' – rather than being Petrea or whoever. As we become accustomed to this, our mind sometimes rebels because we're unused to the feeling of simply 'being'; we might find our body jerks us back into identification with itself or that we get itchy or restless. We can open our eyes if this happens, and then relax back into the practice. There's no rush, so we can be gentle with ourselves as we explore the glories of meditation at our own pace. Gradually we welcome the freedom and liberation that non-identification with body and mind brings as we experience the fullness and power of our creative consciousness.

If meditation is to prove valuable in your life, then give it the priority it deserves. You'll never 'find' time to meditate; you need to 'make' time and you'll only do this if you make it a priority.

You may wonder how you will know if you are meditating. The hallmarks of meditation are that the mind becomes quieter than usual and your breathing is generally very light. If that is your experience, then trust you are meditating.

You can begin your practice by taking some long, slow, deep breaths to help the body to relax, then allow your breathing to return to its natural rhythm. If you have any difficulty with your breathing or with coughing, work comfortably within your own particular limitations or focus your attention on other physical sensations rather than your breathing.

It is preferable to practise meditation sitting comfortably upright in a chair or on the floor. There is a tendency when lying down to fall asleep. This sleep is usually very deep and refreshing, however meditation is about being fully *conscious* and yet deeply relaxed.

If you're seeking to set aside formal times for your meditation practice, then the best times of the day to meditate are at sunrise and sunset when there's a particularly fine energy in the air. However, meditation at any time is better than not doing it at all because you can't manage it at sunrise and / or sunset! It's always best to meditate when your stomach is empty and when you're feeling fresh rather than sleepy. Having a shower to refresh and prepare yourself for meditation can also be very helpful but isn't essential.

You may wish to choose a chair in which to meditate that has adequate support for your head, and allows your feet to rest comfortably flat on the floor. Allow your spine to be comfortably erect so that you're not slouched down into the chair. This is particularly helpful when you're new to meditation and unused to sitting without any support. It's useful to have your body balanced and symmetrical. You may wish to loosen any tight clothing or belts and remove your shoes and glasses. Let your hands rest comfortably in your lap, in a position where they won't slide off and distract you. It's a little like parking a car on a hill: you make sure the wheels are facing the kerb, the handbrake is on and the car is in gear – you park your body in a position where it will not be uncomfortable or distract you from your practice. The less you try in meditation, the better. It is a process only of letting go.

You might like to think of meditation being like the sky and that the thoughts, images and feelings are like clouds drifting through it. Sometimes they're little fluffy white clouds like 'What's for lunch?'

– not that hard to let go of unless you're starving. Other times they're big steely grey clouds like 'I have to sit my final exams next week' – much more difficult to let go of because we want to have a really good panic about it! And before we know it, our world has contracted to that particular group of thoughts and all its associations. We lose the spaciousness of the sky and our world shrinks down to these clouds. However, your job in meditation is to let the thoughts – clouds – go and return to the silence of the clear blue sky.

The sky doesn't endeavour to stop the clouds from passing through. It lets them come, to pass. Likewise in meditation, don't try and stop the thoughts, images or feelings from coming. Simply let them come to pass. In some of your practices there will be a few scattered clouds of thoughts and it will be easy to let them go. At other times your whole inner sky may be full of clouds and you might need to let the thoughts go almost constantly. The fact that you had the awareness to see the thoughts is precisely the point of practising meditation. Don't judge your practice – let each one be sufficient unto itself.

Meditation has been a regular part of my daily life since I discovered its benefits at the age of 17. Years later when I had leukaemia I found that whatever thoughts and feelings I'd been trying to suppress would bubble to the surface during my meditation practice. 'What if I'm not here for Christmas?' 'How will my children cope?' 'How will my parents cope?' 'How will I cope?' 'I wonder who'll come to the funeral.' 'I wonder what they'll say.' 'Who'll be wearing my clothes in two years?' – on and on it would go, and every time I could feel myself going down the emotional gurgler! I could do the same thing over and over again. These same thoughts would repeat themselves endlessly in my mind. I know rats have more brains. In a maze they will go down the same track twice and on finding no cheese will never venture that way again. Me? I'd do the same thing over and over again. It seems, though, that I'm not the only one with this problem, and that many people struggle to keep their thoughts under observation, especially during times of high stress.

Finally I decided to make an 'appointment' with my worries. I said to myself, 'Tomorrow afternoon at four o'clock I'll sit down and have a really good worry.' Next day I sat down at 4 pm, brought myself into the present by connecting with the senses of my body and then consciously invited all my worries and fears to be present. Do you know what happened? Complete silence. That is the nature of worries and fears. They like to sneak in when we're unaware and have their way with us. They have no reality but that which we give them. When we bring the light of our consciousness to them, they evaporate. It can be useful to think of thoughts as creatures floating in the world of mind and that they only have life when we give them our consciousness. Some thoughts are thus enlivened by each of us – this applies both in the lives of individuals as well as in the life of a community or nation.

Computerised imagery is beginning to show some of the biological changes that occur in the brains of people who meditate regularly. It seems that meditation enables the brain to literally rewire itself in positive ways and that negative emotional reactions diminish. This demonstrates that it's not only the physical body that has a natural tendency to heal; our mind is likewise designed to relinquish patterns that are not useful and not borne of our essential nature. In meditation we literally loosen our attachment to our second nature, our acquired nature – the overlayed patterning of the past – and experience the truth of our consciousness, or first nature.

Some people find that having someone guide them through a practice assists in keeping them focused. I have made a meditation practice on CD that is suitable for people wanting such a guide. It's called *Learning to Meditate* and details about ordering it appear in the back of this book.

If we're to experience our own creative source, we need to return to the stillness that is beyond the mind's activity. This silent observer witnesses without judgement, without comment, without preference, without resistance and without aversion. The practice of meditation involves the conscious witnessing of our mind's activity. As soon as we become aware that our consciousness is absorbed by the mind, we let go of the thought, the image, the feeling, and return to witnessing.

The clarity and peace in your mind *after* meditation is what your practice is aiming to achieve. It is this calm and centred state that we continue to practise and prolong so that it infuses every moment of our day. The result of regular meditation is a profoundly heightened awareness in daily life. The richness it brings to our everyday experience is a treasure beyond words and should we lose it, even momentarily, it is sorely missed.

There's a lovely Zen story about the disciple who asked his master, 'Master, how do you put enlightenment into action? How do you practise it in everyday life?' The master replied, 'By eating and by sleeping.' 'But master,' the disciple said, 'everybody sleeps and everybody eats.' The master replied, 'But not everybody eats when they eat and not everybody sleeps when they sleep.'

I trust that with regular practice, the nourishment your spirit receives in meditation will become a treasured gift in your life.

CHAPTER 7

Mind Matters

You are not your mind; you are more than your mind.

Me

My most formidable opponent is a man named Mohandas K. Gandhi. With him I seem to have very little influence.

Mohandas K. Gandhi

I've been through some terrible things in my life, some of which actually happened!

Mark Twain

There are two ways to live your life. One is as though nothing is a miracle. The other is as though everything is a miracle.

Albert Einstein

Environment is more important than willpower.

Me

We love being in the present. It's the juiciest place in life to be. It's where life is unfolding moment by moment. It's where our intuition is heard or felt, where creativity is experienced, where humour and spontaneity reside. The present is where life is, where love is, where creation is unfolding. We cannot experience the presence of life, love or creation in five minutes' time or five minutes ago. We have to be here, now, in order to feel the glory, wonder and possibilities of the present.

However, our minds can create chaos, misery and suffering for us as they jump into the future or into the past; projecting endless possibilities that may never happen as Mark Twain so aptly describes, or regurgitating things from our history and giving life to them in the present.

We go to great lengths to be in the present moment and may even spend a significant proportion of our income on the pursuit of its gifts. Do you think a rock-climber hanging from a cliff is thinking about what she's going to have for dinner? Her body absorbs impressions: her own weight, strength and balance, the wind velocity, the crumbliness of the rocks, the security of the hooks and ropes. She knows exactly where her pinkie is and how much pressure she's got in it! Every sense is heightened because her safety – her life – depends on it. In that state, her mind is focused and absorbed in the detail of maintaining balance and progress towards her goal. The mind is being used *by* her to achieve her goal – to scale the mountain. She's at one with herself, the mountain and her surroundings. It is in such moments that we feel whole, complete and content.

Chances are, if she starts thinking that she forgot to take the chook out of the freezer she'll make a less skilful move and it may well have consequences. Likewise if she allows her mind to be consumed by fears of failure, falling or inadequacy; these thoughts could lead to increased sweating, raised heartbeat, nausea, trembling or her own idiosyncratic ways of manifesting stress – none of which will help her achieve her goal.

This is the same for the windsurfer, the calligrapher, the teacher, the artist, the gardener, the actor, the surgeon, the singer, the mechanic, the musician, the technician, the athlete. Pursuits that require precision and artistry bring the mind to rest, as their focus is on performing the chosen role with excellence. That's why we

admire and enjoy the performance we witness when someone
excels in his or her chosen field. We see the discipline and effort
required for that person to keep focused on the chosen endeavour.
It is a joy to us and indeed nourishes our inner being when we're in
the presence of, or witness the fruits of, such presence of being.
We're touched by the beauty, grace or the perfect execution of a
movement or a brushstroke, or the precision of emphasis or hesitation in music, a song or a speech.

> *Quietness of the mind is master of the deed.*
>
> *Gandhi*

What do we want from our surgeon on the day we go into the operating theatre? In addition to years of experience and excellent
training, what we want on the day is their undivided attention –
their wholehearted presence. It is the gifted surgeon who brings all
of his or her presence to the operating table. *Then* they will recall
everything you've told them and may choose to explore in greater
depth a seemingly minor symptom you mentioned three weeks ago.
Another surgeon might have forgotten that conversation altogether
and sees your case only as a routine procedure, rather than an operation on a person with an individual history. I know a surgeon who
was ridiculed for years because he doesn't allow idle conversation
in the operating theatre and plays meditation chants while he
works. His patients, however, benefit from and value the care his
wholehearted presence brings.

With the abundant harvest that we reap in being present to our
life at every moment comes the realisation that life depends as
much upon our response to its events as upon the events themselves; that each moment is a sufficient end in itself rather than
another step towards some future goal; that it is *now,* in *this
moment* that we sacrifice the glory and wonder that is in and
around us unless we are present to its unfolding potential.

Many years ago I practised the rudiments of calligraphy as a discipline for the mind. My task was to fill an A3 sheet of paper with seven-centimetre-long straight lines, spaced half a centimetre apart, in blocks of ten. The paper was held in place at an angle on an easel. The discipline involved keeping my spine upright, my feet flat on the floor and my arm straight and at eye level while focusing my attention on the space between the ink leaving the nib and the surface of the paper. The only time I changed focus in a half-hour practice was to refill the nib with ink and even then, the same awareness was essential so that I didn't overfill or under-fill the nib. Every time a thought such as, 'What the heck am I bothering with this for?' entered my mind, a little wobble would appear in what was meant to be a straight line. It was fascinating to see the immediate evidence of inattention, of distraction. I devoted half an hour every day to this practice for more than a year before moving on to more complex shapes such as semicircles, ovals, the symbol of infinity and Sanskrit letters.

We are not our mind; we are more than our mind. It is our job to learn how to quieten the mind. If we don't, we generally end up being used *by* our mind. Most of us have had the experience of an overactive mind at 3 am and have had difficulty switching it off. I've heard the mind described as 'a wild drunk monkey swinging through treetops'! Certainly, that's been an accurate description of mine in times past.

Intuition

Intuition is the voice of the non-physical world.

Me

Our intuition is perhaps our least acknowledged but greatest asset. It is the voice of the non-physical world, though it can deliver messages about the physical world. If we train ourselves to discern its voice, it will provide guidance in every moment of our lives. So many of us have quashed our intuition through long neglect of it. It tends to speak in nudges or whispers, dreams, sensations, feelings or images, and is only available when our mind is quiet. Our fears, on the other hand, use the loudspeaker system and so consume our minds that we're sometimes desperate for respite. The voice of love emanates from our creative spirit while fear belongs to the personality, our second nature that we have constructed since our birth. Our intuition is that 'still small voice' that 'knows' rather than 'thinks'.

Fears propel the mind with thoughts of Will I? / Won't I?, Should I? / Shouldn't I?, Can I? / Can't I? Our intuition, however, knows precisely what to do or say, knows how to 'be', and whether something is true for us or not. Peter Russell describes intuition as our 'inner tuitions'.

Some people talk of a 'gut feeling' or they say, 'I know it in my heart,' or that something 'feels' right. Some people talk of having hunches or receiving nudges. Intuition has long been ridiculed and we've been indoctrinated to not trust its wisdom. But it is time to recognise that intuition is a valid source of information. We need to train our intellect to listen to and express the intuitive voice. When we follow our intuition our lives have an increased joy, spontaneity, humour and sense of aliveness. It feels like more life flows through us.

As you read this book your intuition will give you the nudge if what you read resonates with your own sense of things. If it does, excellent – take the information on board and use it. If it doesn't, excellent – leave it aside for later reflection or let it go. No-one knows you better than you do. Trust that you'll recognise what is of value to you when you see, hear or feel it. Don't believe a word you read or hear if it doesn't resonate with your own inner sense of things.

Our intuition can give us valuable information about what's going on in our body even before a noticeable symptom appears. Countless people have told me they had an intuitive sense that something needed attention long before being diagnosed with their illness or with its recurrence. Don't give your power away to someone else because they're the so-called expert. *You* are the expert on you. Find someone who'll listen and respect your perspective.

Many people, of which the majority were women, have told me that their doctors have accused them of being hypochondriacs or malingerers because they've returned again and again with more than a suspicion that something wasn't right in their body. A delay in diagnosis can result in anguish for the person plus the consequences of a delay in treatment.

Our intuition doesn't only tell us if our body isn't well – it can also bring us other information and surprises, as Christine's story illustrates.

Christine had been experiencing pain in several parts of her body and finally went to a doctor to find the cause. She'd virtually 'forgotten' or repressed memories of having had a mastectomy for breast cancer a number of years earlier. She didn't mention that she'd had cancer to her doctor until he discovered her mastectomy. Subsequent tests confirmed that not only had the breast cancer recurred, it had already advanced extensively into her bones and lungs. Though immediate chemotherapy was strongly recommended by her doctor, Christine hesitated to agree to having treatment. Her oncologist suggested she get counselling and recommended she see me.

Christine was aged in her late thirties and looked as if she might have packed a lot of living into those years. Her body was small and nuggety and bore several visible scars.

Christine had developed a fierce independence to protect and conceal her real feelings. Love, gentleness and tenderness had never played a part in her upbringing or life, and she'd learned to survive in a tough world. She'd had relationships that were physically abusive at worst, having lost several teeth in fights, and emotionally unsustaining at best.

Though consumption of drugs and alcohol had been a large part of her past, she'd made real and positive changes in her life for the better. For nearly two years she'd been drug and alcohol free, and had recently ended a relationship with a man who'd been very dependent on her. She treasured the solitude and peace she felt in her small housing commission flat – her first real home – and she was deriving much pleasure from feathering her nest – something she'd never done before.

Christine was confused. She didn't understand why she was so adamant about not having chemotherapy. We explored her beliefs and feelings about her life, cancer and chemotherapy, yet nothing jumped out as a reason for her hesitation. Christine wasn't philosophically opposed to having drug treatment and she wasn't afraid of the side effects they might induce. She reckoned she'd had plenty of experience dealing with the side effects of non-prescription drugs and that chemotherapy, in her mind, would probably be a breeze in comparison! She said chemotherapy just didn't feel right for her at this time, but she was quite open to reviewing her decision later. She even refused pain medication because it didn't feel right. She said that since being drug and alcohol free, she'd been enjoying being alive for the first time and feeling everything was important to her.

Christine seemed apprehensive about telling the doctor of her decision to postpone chemotherapy for a few weeks. She thought she'd have to change doctors even though she'd liked him. He'd told her that treatment would extend her life, but wouldn't cure her. Christine was afraid that he'd be angry with her if she decided against his advice. She felt her cancer had clearly been there for some time and that, regardless of the consequences, she needed to honour what felt right for her.

Actually fronting up to her doctor and telling him these things was a major challenge for Christine, so we discussed how she might approach it. Men had always been problematic for her. Her father had been a violent alcoholic who used emotional blackmail and physical punishment as a daily strategy until his death when she was 12. Christine said she'd learned early that if she was bossy or 'knew best' when it came to interactions with men, especially those in power, she could cope with them. It had been her way of equalising the relationship. After all, she'd been hit by plenty of men and had come to respect their anger and physical size.

At this point in her life, Christine no longer wanted to perpetuate this unhealthy pattern. She recognised that it was a defence she'd developed against feeling emotionally vulnerable. Since she'd removed herself from the negative environment of drug, alcohol and physical abuse, and began attending a 12-step program, she'd started to enjoy the process of understanding herself and expressing her feelings in a more positive way.

Christine decided that rather than going to see her doctor and risking a confrontation over her decision not to start treatment, she'd write him a letter to let him know of her choice. She worked and reworked the letter before she sent it, as it was important to her that it conveyed her real feelings and did not seem she was just fobbing him off. Contrary to the assumptions she'd made about what his response would be, the doctor rang to let her know he appreciated her decision and would see her again when she was ready.

Christine also decided to join the Quest for Life Centre cancer support group as there were some particular issues around having cancer that she didn't feel were relevant to her 12-step companions. She became a regular member of the group and we were inspired by her willingness to heal every aspect of her life. Her ruthless self-honesty gave courage and inspiration to everyone present.

During the first weeks of her attendance at the group her abdomen began to swell. Believing it was probably due to the cancer's spread, and still reluctant to return to her doctor in case he pressured her to commence chemotherapy, Christine chose to ignore it. However, when her clothes became uncomfortably tight, she realised that to deny what was going on simply wasn't helpful. She reluctantly returned to her oncologist.

As it turned out, Christine's need to listen to herself and honour the truth of what she felt was exactly what she'd needed to do. Two months after her decision not to commence treatment she found that she was more than four months pregnant with twins. Had she begun the chemotherapy at the recommended time it would certainly have damaged her growing babies.

When Christine told the cancer support group her news we celebrated with her. She was convinced that if these little ones had come to *her*, given her wild history, then she wanted to provide them with the very best start in life she could. Christine made fresh juices for herself and the babies every day and made sure her diet was full of the right nutrients for them all. She used to say, 'These kids must be real desperados to come to the likes of me and I'm going to give them the best start possible.'

Christine chose to continue her pregnancy until the babies were able to survive outside of her body. This time of balancing her illness with creating a loving and nurturing environment for her growing babies saw all the hardness go out of Christine. She felt the miracle of this pregnancy and the blessing the babies were to her long before their birth. Though her body struggled with the cancer, it did not progress as fast as it might have, and she was able to carry her babies until she was seven months pregnant. After the birth, and when Christine was physically very depleted, she began her cancer treatment.

The joy she received from both her pregnancy and the arrival of her children filled her with a peace she'd never known before. During this time, Christine met a kind and generous man who delighted in taking care of all three of them. Gary couldn't have been a gentler or more loving companion to her and father to them. He, too, had had a challenging life involving drugs and alcohol but, like Christine, he had found his healing. Christine and Gary often wept together about the future as her illness progressed and yet laughter was never far behind their tears.

Christine died peacefully in Gary's arms with her four-year-old twins by her side. Given the extent of her disease and the additional challenge of pregnancy, Christine lived far longer than anyone but she and Gary could have imagined.

Life is not about wrong or right, shoulds or shouldn'ts. Life can be lived with love and compassion for others and ourselves, knowing that life / love is eternal and that the physical body provides the means by which we experience our humanity.

The incessant chatter that goes on in our mind often stops us from experiencing the possibilities in each present moment. In order for us to hear our intuition, our mind must be quiet and present.

For instance, imagine you're walking to the local pharmacy ten minutes' away to purchase some goods. While you're walking, your mind chatters on. Perhaps you're thinking about your woeful financial situation or you're worrying about your kids, rehashing a recent argument, fretting over your relationship, resenting your job, feeling sad about unresolved childhood issues or preoccupied with your plans for the future. You arrive at the pharmacy. You've forgotten why you went there. In the shop, you've got no interest or energy to engage with the person on the other side of the counter, let alone enquire about her day, because you're so preoccupied with your own problems. You avoid eye contact. You grab a box of tissues because you're bound to need those and you walk home again worrying about the future, fretting about the past, frustrated with your kids, resenting your job, rehashing conversations or arguments, and so on. Have you ever made a trip like that? It seems that many of us live much of our life like that!

What you've done in the time you've walked from home to the pharmacy and back again is secrete a chemical cocktail in your brain and other parts of your body in response to whatever your awareness has been focused on. If you've been preoccupied with regrets, recriminations, worry, bitterness, anxiety, fears, uncertainties, resentment, rehashing past events or projecting your worries, fears, concerns and dread into the future, you've also been producing the chemicals of the feelings you've experienced.

There's another way to walk to the pharmacy. You're over your childhood because you've cried about it, written about it, talked about it or done whatever you needed to in order for those events to be in your history rather than nibbling at your present. In this way you have forgiven yourself, others and life. You've got your finances under control because that's your responsibility. You're in the best of relationships because you know a good one needs daily attention. You know you've given your children the best start in life you were able to given who you are, what has happened to you and what you made of it, and can set them free to create a life for themselves. You know that worrying about the future changes nothing (except your biology!). Then, you're simply free to walk.

You hear the crunch of the gravel beneath your feet. You notice how your body feels as you walk and you notice if anything feels any different. You feel the touch of the air against your cheeks and catch the waft of blossom floating by. You see the flurry of petals set dancing by the breezes. You relish the play of light and shadow. You hear the laughter of children and birdsong. You connect with the dog that tried to give you a smile. You enjoy every breath as it flows effortlessly in and out of your body. You arrive at the pharmacy. You've got boundless energy to greet the assistant and perhaps brighten her day. You know exactly why you're there and you get your goods and walk home enjoying the sights, sounds, smells and feelings of simply being alive. It's as if you see life winking at you everywhere.

Outwardly, this second way of walking might look identical to the first, but your experience of it is completely different. This second way of walking produces a very different physiology. You've secreted the chemicals of peace, contentment, joy or even bliss. Because, why not?

Our walking is not just a way of reaching our destination but a rich journey in itself. It's often at these times, when the mind is open and receptive to receiving the messages from our senses, that our intuition operates. Messages pop into our mind – they might be as simple as a reminder to ring someone or to read a particular book or to visit somewhere – but they're important messages from a deeper, more aware part of our being.

If we've been trying to figure out a problem or find a solution to a situation, these are precisely the times when our intuition is likely to give some pointers, or indeed the entire answer – those 'Aha!' moments of understanding or recognition. These moments might occur while we're showering, sitting idle at traffic lights, or involved in any of our daily routines like washing up the dishes, cleaning the bathtub, brushing our teeth or taking out the rubbish, or when the mind is quiet and receptive – perhaps in the presence of music or nature. It is often when the mind is 'idling', not thinking about anything in particular, that these intuitive thoughts are experienced. We suddenly 'get' the idea that we should visit a particular person or place (for no apparent reason), go to the shelf for a particular book, revisit a conversation in which we realise we were misunderstood, or whatever.

It is the unresolved issues in our mind that take us away from experiencing this present moment in all its glory and block our intuition from being heard.

Science continues to discover new hormones and chemicals that act as neurotransmitters. These chemical messengers are constantly tweaking our cells' performance. One of the hormones that we secrete has been named anandamide, also known as the bliss hormone – *ananda* being a Sanskrit word meaning bliss. When this hormone locks onto a receptor that's present on billions of our cells, it gives a positive message that encourage the cell to optimise its performance. Anandamide is part of our body's internal pharmacy of hormones and chemicals designed to improve and maintain our health. Why wouldn't our body secrete self-healing, health-maintaining hormones and chemicals to help fulfil its purpose – to house the spirit that is here to be realised?

We need to honour and listen to the wise inner voice of our intuition because it is one of our greatest assets in life. It is the voice of our creative spirit and the guiding light for our journey to full consciousness. It is in the presence of this intuitive self that we feel a deep sense of connectedness to that which is sacred within us.

When we find ourselves in a pickle – we've married the wrong person, chosen a career that doesn't satisfy us, got ourselves in a flap over being late, or whatever – nearly always we can look back and see that our intuition gave us a nudge or two which we chose to ignore. Some people have walked down the aisle *knowing* it wasn't a good idea but saying inwardly, 'I *will* make this work!' In so doing, we even say to ourselves that we know we are committed by 'will' rather than by love.

Some people, as mentioned in Greg's story, have made business decisions based on good cheer and a handshake only to find that both parties had a very different perspective – each, of course, convinced that theirs was right. Their intuition might well have suggested that it would be best to get the agreement down in writing, but they dismissed this formality as unnecessary.

We can live our entire life by listening to this wise inner voice of our spirit, which has a different quality to the voice of our fears and judgements. This wise inner voice always leads us towards the highest in us, the greatest in us, and does not criticise or diminish us; it does not see us in terms of 'better than' or 'worse than' – both states of mind that serve to separate us from one another.

While ever the mind is projecting its fears, hopes, fantasies, frustrations, anxieties and worries into the future or is absorbed in resentments, rehashing, blaming, bitterness and regrets from the past, we stifle our ability to hear the wise voice of our spirit. This voice can only be heard in the present and only when the mind is quiet.

I'm sure research will show, if it hasn't already, that our intuition – or this inner wisdom – is only available to us when the mind is quiet, which in turn is dependent on the chemical and electrical state of the brain. Only then is the brain receptive to making previously unmade connections or able to interpret information from within and outside of itself. I suspect chemicals and hormones, oxytocin amongst them, will be implicated in this ability and it will no longer be seen as something psychic or strange.

We all have the ability to be intuitive. The more we're willing to be guided by our intuition the more clearly we hear its voice. The more we ignore our intuition and stifle it through doubting, worrying, fearing, regretting, resenting and so on, the less we have access to it, until finally it is no longer evident in our experience. By learning to contact, listen to and act on our intuition, we can connect directly to this inner wisdom and allow it to become our guiding force.

If there are problems in our life, the universe is endeavouring to show us something. And instead of asking, 'Why did this happen?' we can turn our attention inside and ask for clarity expressed in an attitude of: 'Help me to understand what is happening here.' Endlessly chewing over the reasons why in our rational mind usually leads us into more turmoil. But we can quieten the mind and ask the voice of our heart to be heard instead. The answer usually comes to us in quiet reflection and not through the argumentativeness of the mind. After asking for clarity from within, we may rely on a sense of what feels right for us and act on that. Sometimes our answer is delivered to us through a person, a situation, or something we hear, read, see or dream. If we train ourselves to be aware of our intuition, we will see its evidence everywhere.

Our denial of our intuition is driven by our fear of it and a lack of trust in ourselves. Intuition is simply a way for us to increase our consciousness and effectiveness by non-rational means.

Recent research has evaluated intelligence tests for the past 100 years and has shown an interesting growth in one particular area of human intelligence. Each successive generation has considerably increased its ability to think laterally. Lateral thinking allows us to arrive at an accurate conclusion without going through the logical steps to achieve that knowing. This, to me, is the same as our intuitive abilities as our intuition allows us to know something without thinking it through.

This inner wisdom – the ability to read our immediate environment with clear discernment – can be extremely helpful. Imagine your car has broken down on an isolated stretch of road in an unfamiliar area. Your mobile phone is out of range and you have no way of calling for help. Don't you want to be able to accurately discern the qualities of the person who stops to pick you up? Do you jump into the first car that pulls up? Or do you have your inner antenna at work to discern whether this driver has honourable intentions and is a person you're willing to trust? If we simply jump into situations without using our inner antenna as well as listening to and trusting our intuition, we may well find ourselves in situations that bring us regret.

The Inner Antenna

Different in nature from our intuition, the inner antenna is the part of our mind that is seeking to find information about things we're interested in.

For instance, for those of us who've ever been pregnant, didn't we see pregnant women everywhere? When we buy a new blue car, we notice every car of the same model and colour, and we seem to see them everywhere. For those of us who've ever been on crutches, didn't we connect with all the people who were limping, in wheelchairs, on walking sticks, on crutches? There may even have been a wink and a nod of recognition as we passed complete strangers having a common experience, in this case feeling mutually physically incapacitated in the leg department.

A friend of mine once shared a lovely story about her inner antenna at work. Lyn had recently purchased a popular new model of car in a mauve-grey colour. While driving with her partner, she noticed an identical model ahead and sped up to draw alongside it. 'Look, that car's exactly the same as mine!' she exclaimed. She blew the horn and waved enthusiastically at the driver who stared blankly back at her. Then her partner quietly pointed out, 'Perhaps they don't realise we're in my car and that yours is at home in the carport.' At which point Lyn shot off like a rocket so that she'd completely lose the other driver, and escape her embarrassment. The mere mention of the incident has precipitated hilarity ever since.

Our inner antenna works in another way, too. Imagine we've emerged from our childhood with the belief that we don't fit in, that we'll never really belong. It has become second nature to us to see an inhospitable world that makes no place for us. Our inner antenna will be hard at work scanning every experience in life to reassure us that what we believe to be true about ourselves is so. In situation after situation we perceive that we've been left out, not invited, overlooked or not included, and our inner antenna will grab that information to verify the belief we hold about life or about ourselves, and thus it is maintained.

If this is our belief, we'll experience emotional pain whenever we feel similarly threatened – perhaps when we're overlooked for a promotion, not invited to a friend's gathering, our new hairstyle is not mentioned and so on. All these situations will engage the neural network of previously felt emotions about being separate from other people, different from them or less or more than other people.

We unconsciously set ourselves up to re-experience the pain because it is second nature to us to feel that way. So, in the hairstyle example, instead of us being able to lightheartedly say, 'What do you think of my new hair do?' we are more likely to see it as another opportunity to verify our belief that no-one will notice. We set an 'exam' for other people; we'll examine again whether our belief is right. If we feel comfortable with ourselves then other people's opinion of us will not be taken personally.

Imagine emerging from our childhood believing that we are superior to most through our intellect, wealth, education, social standing or whatever it was our family valued. These feelings give us a sense of being separate from other people, perhaps even better than other people. Likewise, to emerge from a childhood where we believe we are inferior to others because of the feelings we've experienced through our lack of wealth, encouragement, education, social standing or accolades also leads us to believe we are separate from other people. Life will continue to bring us circumstances that stir the long-held feelings around our emotional wounds. These are the opportunities to release ourselves from the grip of erroneous beliefs about who we are, in our essence.

Imagine we have a teenager who we feel is drifting away from us, or who is engaging in risky behaviours. Our internal antenna has brought to our attention some unsettling information; perhaps there has been a lack of eye contact lately, or a change in appearance or personal hygiene, or he or she is no longer engaging in conversation with ease or is spending longer periods in moody isolation in their bedroom. It might be that his or her reasons or excuses sound lame and they don't ring true. A flag goes up in our mind.

This flag's appearance, however momentary, is of vital importance. Once our internal antenna has gathered information, our intuition will evaluate the information and alert us to explore further.

We need to use our inner antenna to weigh up encounters, people and conversations and notice if they feel right for us; whether they resonate with our own commonsense and reasoning. The problem is that many of us have lost faith in our own commonsense and indeed have been convinced to doubt the commonsense answer unless it's been scientifically proven!

We may choose to ignore the information our inner antenna brings us and experience the consequences, or listen to it and find the problem, if there is one: mismatching values, an unspoken expectation, missing honesty, unchecked assumptions and so on. If a problem is found, we have new and valuable information on which to base our next decision, conversation or course of action.

If we continually ignore such flags in our mind they'll no longer present themselves to be heeded. If we don't use our intuition, we lose it. By cultivating awareness we can be conscious, moment to moment, of our intuition's nudges. Our internal antenna gathers information about whatever we're interested in, and our intuition evaluates and prompts us to explore further, if necessary.

Let's return to our teenager. Our antenna has brought us information and our intuition prompts us to enquire further. At this point, one of two possibilities generally occurs: we either react from our fears, borne of our unresolved emotional history, or we're able to make an appropriate response to the situation.

For instance, perhaps we are fearful of what we might find if we ask questions or seek clarification about his or her behaviour. Perhaps we feel incompetent to deal with what we might find. We may be weighed down by our own insecurities or worries and placate ourselves with an inner dialogue of hollow words that bring little comfort. We might reassure ourselves that their behaviour is normal or typical of their age group. Our insecurities and fears may impel us to react by placing more stringent boundaries around our teenager without understanding, discussion or resolution of the underlying issues. Our fears may stop us from listening to our intuition.

The alternative is to respond to our son or daughter with an open heart and a clear mind, without the distraction of fear. Such situations give us the opportunity to heal our insecurities and fears, to bring them to awareness, without reacting from them. If we don't do this, we continue to react from our beliefs about life or ourselves that have been laid down in us as second nature. The reactivation of these feelings does not allow us to access solutions, wisdom, humour or spontaneity because our consciousness is absorbed by our reactivated feelings instead. When we *respond* to our teenager, rather than react, we are more likely to find a way to communicate effectively, re-establishing trust and connectedness and maintain the solidarity of our relationship.

Whatever our beliefs about ourselves might be, our inner antenna will be seeking to verify and maintain them. If we fear that we're ageing more quickly than others, that we're poorer or richer than everyone we know, that we're prettier or uglier, that we're smarter or dumber, fatter or thinner, more or less athletic or healthy, happier or more miserable, then be assured, our inner antenna will be hard at work making comparisons to confirm that which we believe to be so – and we'll see evidence to back up our belief time after time. Whatever we believe to be true, we're right!

It is a blessing to reach a time in our life where we say, 'That's it! I'm no longer willing to allow my reality to be dictated to me by the unhelpful beliefs I've gathered in the past.' In that magic moment, it is possible to change our experience of reality to one that supports us in achieving peace of mind.

Most of us have come to that point in some situation. It might have been when we were 'over' a relationship, habit or addiction, or a town, or job, or a reactive way of relating to someone we love. We'd well and truly milked the juice out of that experience and it wasn't satisfying us any longer.

It's a wonderful point to reach where we can say decisively, 'That's it! Enough. I'm done with this.' In that moment, our life can change.

If we change what we believe about life, our life will change. We create our reality with our beliefs and intentions. In each moment, we either consciously choose our response or we react from our beliefs. If we react unconsciously, we evolve unconsciously. If we choose consciously, we evolve consciously. What stands between us and a different life is a matter of responsible choice.

As I have said previously and emphasise frequently because it is so important, once we want peace more than anything – more than being right; more than blame or resentment; more than the endless cycle of being more than / less than; a cure, anger, despair or endless grief; more than anything at all – the whole universe conspires to bring it about and we begin to find the stepping stones to our pure consciousness. People, seminars, books, interviews, classes and more come our way to facilitate our awakening consciousness.

If we attach our sense of self to how we look, we may not take the ageing process well. If we attach our sense of self to what we do, then who are we and what is our value when our 'doing' is stripped away from us through outer events, illness or the unforeseen?

Our creative spirit is our wellspring, source, essence, inner being, soul, higher self – however you like to think of it. It is, after all, beyond naming. Our consciousness is the wellspring of joy, wisdom, clarity, love and what is sacred and divine. When yearning for union with consciousness overtakes all else, everything in our life begins to fall into place.

That doesn't mean life gets less colourful and the unexpected, the unthinkable or the unimagined won't happen. It does mean that when those things do happen we view them quite differently and they have far less capacity to rob us of peace.

We anchor our sense of self in that which is beyond the vagaries of change and we find peace in the midst of pain, in the midst of the unexpected. Pain is a feeling and an experience while suffering is a point of view. Peace becomes our beginning and ending place, and our sense of equilibrium is not easily shaken.

A Vietnam veteran who attended one of our Quest for Life Centre programs had had a long history of bitterness and rage. He was angry and resentful about the fact that his name had come up in the ballot to go to the war, and that after his experiences of losing friends and suffering physically in the war, he'd returned to a country that he felt didn't value his contribution. He blamed the government, the war and the community for his despair and depression.

During the program, however, he discovered many things that he valued and respected about himself, and on the final day he said, 'I've just realised that nothing wrong has ever happened in my life. I wouldn't be who I am now – I wouldn't be sitting here with all of you [participants] – if every step towards this place hadn't happened.'

We don't heal *from* something we resist or fear, we heal *into* that which we more deeply desire. Healing requires that we're willing to examine every belief, judgement, value, desire, inhibition, expectation and assumption we hold. In time, we discard everything but those things that we find true in their depths.

Once the lid is off our own Pandora's box of inner deliberations, there's no putting it back on. In other words, once the voice of consciousness has called us back to experience itself, it will demand that we nurture and follow the path until we discover a truer representation of our essence and create an environment in which we can live an inner and outer life that is congruent with what we know to be true in our core.

Healing Versus Curing

Milton Erickson says that healing involves a change in perception about the memories and events of our lives, and those we have perceived as limiting or negative can become a valuable resource for growth, wisdom and understanding. When asked how he developed his powerful observation skills he replied, 'Oh, I was luckier than most. I was paralysed as a young man so I got to lie around and study people for quite some time.'

When we engage our problem-solving thinking processes to aim for a cure, we're not listening to our intuition but just focusing on ridding ourselves of something. Yet life is a process of unfolding rather than a finite state that we achieve, and curing is only about the finite state, not the process.

Healing addresses the whole person and takes into account the physical, mental, emotional and spiritual aspects, thus leading to a deeper understanding of and wisdom about ourselves. After all, life is not a competition to see who stays alive the longest. We value a life by the passion with which it was lived, by the love made evident and by the peace or joy given to others, rather than its length.

In modern medicine, a cure is normally defined as an external medical intervention that reliably removes physical disease in most people. Healing, in contrast, is an inner movement towards wholeness that can take place at physical, emotional, mental and spiritual levels. Most ancient healing traditions place their primary emphasis on this inner healing – on caring for the human soul – rather than on curing.

You may want to remind yourself of the Four Cs, outlined earlier, as a definition of peace.

- We regain a sense of **control**, choosing not to react from our history but making an appropriate response to the situation in which we find ourselves. This requires awareness and a desire to participate rather than feeling like a helpless victim of our circumstances.

- We care enough to be **committed** to getting emotionally up to date with our life, so that we can be here now – in the present moment.

- We find our life positively **challenging**, recognising that we're here to grow in wisdom and in our capacity to love, and that our suffering has meaning for us.

- We feel lovingly **connected** to those with whom we share our life and to our own spirit.

When we desire to live with this sense of peace in our lives, the outcome is guaranteed. Peace is always possible and, regardless of the circumstances of our lives, it becomes our reality.

Keeping Good Company

The habitual thoughts, patterns, assumptions, expectations, beliefs and behaviours we've accumulated will keep us stuck unless we're willing to have things be different. If we want to liberate ourselves from that which would keep us bound, then we need two things: a willingness for things to be different and an environment that supports the changes we desire.

It is essential to keep our minds in good company – that which uplifts and supports us in moving in the direction of our spirit rather than in the direction of our fears or negative or self-defeating behaviours and beliefs. This not only involves the people we share our life with but it also includes the books we read, the television programs and movies we watch, the music we listen to, the environments we enter and the activities we engage in.

Environment is more important than willpower. We do need willpower, but alone it is generally insufficient if we continue to re-enter the same environment that supports our negativity, fears or habitual behaviours. Change requires an effort of will *and* a supportive environment.

In this regard, our family can be part of the problem. We may have developed ways of relating to one another that keep us all stuck on the hurdy-gurdy of habitual reactions. Words or phrases that this family might frequently use would include: 'He never . . .', 'If only . . .', 'You always . . .', 'She should . . .', 'I can't . . .', 'He ought . . .', 'I have to . . .', 'You must . . .' and so on. This is the language belonging to the victim mentality mentioned previously. In such situations, the family of our blood is rarely the family of our spirit! It is a bonus if our families honour and respect our growth and change, and something, if it is the case, for which to be very grateful.

Some families mature from those born of blood to our spiritual family through suffering and facing significant challenges together. Such family bonds of love, trust and deep respect for one another are treasures indeed. For many people though, their spiritual family will be gathered through life. These are the people we choose as our companions and friends and who celebrate our growth and development in consciousness and will not diminish our efforts or deliberately trample on our vulnerabilities.

The things in life that cause us greatest anguish and pain are generally the very things that also cause us to know ourselves deeply. These painful treasures become our pearls. Remember, the pearl only comes about in the oyster because something irritated the heck out of the oyster. That which causes us greatest irritation or anguish is the very means by which we get to explore parts of ourselves that we would never have ventured into otherwise.

In this way, our suffering becomes meaningful. It breaks us open to understanding the realms of despair, love, panic, fear, joy, self-loathing or whatever may be particular to us as individuals. It enables us to bring some light into the darkness and to understand and know ourselves in our depths. It makes us better companions to those who likewise suffer and we no longer shrink from their company because we don't know what to do or say.

It doesn't mean that we ever know what it's like for another person and therefore to say, 'I know exactly how you feel,' is generally never appropriate, or even true. This is so even between people who love each other dearly and whose suffering stems from the same cause.

For instance, a couple whose child is killed in an accident will probably have very different experiences of grief. This may well involve different timing, too. On any one day, one partner may be feeling a whole gamut of emotions that are completely different to the other's experience. Unless there's enough love, space, trust and communication within the relationship, there's a good chance that such an event will break not only their hearts but also the bonds of the relationship. Indeed, in a healthy relationship where there's love, trust, space and communication, such an event will allow hearts to break open and grieving to occur that make the bonds inherent in friendship and respect even stronger.

What we *can* know, and probably won't need to say is, 'I know how that place feels for me and I'm willing to be with you while you're in that place in yourself.'

The level to which we're willing to experience our own pain, fear, despair, panic, love, joy or any other emotion is the level to which we'll be able to join with others in their own explorations. If we cannot go near our fears or our despair or indeed, our love, then we won't want to be around those who are having their own experience of those emotions. We may well disappear when some tragedy strikes someone we know because we've never confronted the unthinkable in our own life. Or, in another instance, we might sabotage loving relationships because we're unwilling to trust another's love.

We cannot presume to know another's pain; we can only ever experience our own. However, our willingness to be present with another person and to accompany them in their journey into their own darkness is a gift in itself. To shed the light of our presence and the wisdom gained from venturing into our own darkness is often sufficient to illuminate the way for another.

What is to give light must first endure burning.

Viktor Frankl

Returning to the pearls for a moment, it is also wise to respect those things that have caused us pain, angst and anguish – our pearls. Do not place your pearls before swine! In this regard, swine are those people who would mock you, trivialise your pearls, laugh at them or use them as a weapon against you at a later time.

Share your pearls only with people who will honour them and treat them with the respect they deserve. They are your path home to your own pure consciousness, your creative essence. Treat them honourably and they will serve their purpose well.

The mind is its own place, and in itself can make a heaven of hell, a hell of heaven.

John Milton

Learn to get in touch with the silence within yourself and know that everything in life has a purpose.

Elizabeth Kübler-Ross

Learning to manage the mind in a way that supports us in living in the present can be our aim. Much of our suffering is caused by an overactive and unmanaged mind. It's forever jumping into the future or into our unresolved recent or distant past. Our minds are then full of the hopes, fears, expectations, assumptions, fantasies and worries about what might happen, could happen and probably won't happen; or they're absorbed by regrets, longings, resentment, blame, bitterness, re-livings, guilt, shame or recriminations.

We all talk about our mind as if it were a separate part of ourselves. We say, 'I'll keep it in mind' as if it were a receptacle into which we deposit ideas. We say, 'He lost his mind' to describe behaviour that lacks reason. We say, 'I can't bring it to mind' because we know this to be one of the embarrassing failings of the 'mind' – after all, *we'd* never forget! We accuse others of having a 'closed mind' when they're unable to take on new ideas. We talk of a 'mind-set' that encompasses a group of ideas underpinning a belief. We've got our minds set on our goals for the future. We change our minds if we see reason to or we're in two minds if we can't.

The greatest revolution of our generation is the discovery that human beings, by changing the inner attitudes of their minds, can change the outer aspects of their lives.

William James

Once we understand how our beliefs dictate their consequences, we can become more conscious of what we choose to hold dear. This embodies a tremendous point of power. We realise that we are the creators of our own reality and that with love, flexibility, humour and creativity we can change our perceptions and experience to that which demonstrates peace.

CHAPTER 8

Emotional Matters

You are not your emotions, you are more than your emotions.

Me

People travel to wonder at the height of mountains,
At the huge waves of the sea, at the long courses of
rivers, at the vast compass of the ocean, at the
circular motion of the stars;
And they pass by themselves without wondering.

St Augustine

In the final analysis
the hope of every person
is simply peace of mind.

Dalai Lama

We frequently identify closely with our feelings, perhaps even more closely than with our thoughts. Yet we're often afraid to explore our feelings because we believe it might entail the reopening of old wounds that we'd rather keep in the background of our life.

We value mental abilities highly in our society and often fear the emotional realm because it can be messy or make us feel vulnerable or out of control. However, emotional healing is essential if we're to live in the present and have peace of mind. Healing in our emotional world allows us to get up to date with our life so that we live with increasing wisdom and compassion. We no longer react from the emotional wounds of the past but have brought them to consciousness and released ourselves from their influence. In this way we can liberate ourselves from the bonds of the past.

We don't have to go fossicking around in our history in order to find these emotional wounds. Whatever is unresolved from the past will appear in the present again and again until we find a way of healing it. By witnessing our reactions to present-time events we become aware of these past wounds and have the opportunity to either transform them or give them expression.

Our physical body is designed to self-heal. When we cut or injure our body, it automatically activates the healing process in the wounded area. We don't have to do anything; our body has an innate wisdom about healing. Likewise with the healing of our emotions; life will continue to bring us experiences that provide the opportunity to heal our emotional wounds. There is a natural tendency to move towards wholeness, healing and self-realisation. This tendency is what motivates and moves us toward enquiry and seeking to realise the essence of who we are.

Our feelings are messages from a deeper place within us. If we ignore one message, another will come, and another, until we heed its presence. Once we see this in operation in our lives, we realise that nothing 'wrong' or 'bad' is happening and that every moment is an opportunity to be aware and present so that we can make appropriate responses to life's challenges. Then we can embrace the vulnerable parts of ourselves instead of living in fear of them. It is not the world that needs changing but our response to the world. Experience is not what happens to us. It is what we do with what happens to us that makes it a useful experience in our journey towards wholeness.

It isn't always easy to change how we see reality. We don't need to change ourselves, others or the world. We need to change our perceptions of ourselves, others and the world. Obviously this is not as easy as it sounds. When we have any kind of pain in our life, be it physical, mental, emotional or spiritual, we automatically tense up, resist the pain and / or fight it. We complain about the pain.

Rarely do we accept the pain and ask, 'What is this pain all about; why am I having this pain?' Resisting the pain makes it more intense. Accepting the pain and working through it paradoxically resolves it. And in its place is a lesson in our lives. Then we can perceive the pain not as a punishment but as a communication that tells us something needs an adjustment. It demands of us a new awareness. Instead of resisting, as we have done before, we open our hearts in compassion and our previous defences are no longer needed. Our job is to be aware rather than to react. Reactions are borne of our unhealed emotional history while a response becomes possible when the wisdom is gleaned from our emotional history but no longer defines us or negatively influences our actions.

The need for this emotional healing becomes more urgent when we're confronted with our mortality or if some other unforeseen event occurs. Many people don't realise that when we're dealing with grief, trauma or tragedy, we're likely to also be confronted with the unresolved issues of our lifetime. This can take people completely by surprise. They wonder why they're preoccupied with past traumas in addition to the present one.

This comes about because the present trauma chemically and electrically activates in our brain and body other similar unresolved feelings from past traumas. These unresolved issues are literally stored in our tissues and are brought into our awareness whenever we're in the presence of a feeling that reactivates the chemicals, hormones and neural pathways associated with feeling that way.

This is particularly noticeable with grief. When we're grieving for a recent, and sometimes not-so-recent, loss we also deal again with any previous losses that we might have suffered. It is also common for people who are grieving to experience some of the physical symptoms that their loved one had, particularly at the time of anniversaries (of marriage, birthdays or date of death) or other significant occasions. I've known many grieving people who've undergone all kinds of medical diagnostic tests to find out 'what's wrong' with them. More often than not, the tests proved negative though that doesn't at all imply that the symptoms are not physical and very real. The symptoms are often particularly present in the month leading up to one of these anniversaries or occasions. It can be useful to be aware of this fact and build in some other supports around this time, as the following story illustrates.

Barbara experienced a crippling migraine on the same date in the month that her husband George had died of a cerebral haemorrhage. She'd rarely had migraines in her life and, due to the shock that she experienced at the suddenness of George's death, she hadn't noticed the relationship between the date of the month of this event and her migraines. Barbara's migraine even started in the same area that her husband's cerebral haemorrhage had occurred.

Barbara had a fairly high-powered job and she'd thrown herself back into it with gusto after George's death. She hadn't allowed herself much time to grieve and take on board the reality of his absence and the profound sadness of missing him. Their daughter, Laura, was intellectually disabled and required dropping off and picking up each day at her nearby carer and George, of course, was no longer able to help with this. Barbara felt she would have to keep everything 'together' otherwise she'd 'fall in a heap' and where would that leave her and Laura? She hadn't talked in depth to Laura about George's death because she was unsure of how helpful it might be to either of them.

Once she was able to make the connection between the migraines and the date of George's death, Barbara put in place a few changes.

She didn't schedule any challenging activities or appointments during the anniversary week of George's death. Instead she went for a walk in the mornings on their favourite track after she'd dropped Laura off for the day, and had a warm bath each of the three nights before his monthly anniversary. Barbara had a massage a couple of days before the day of the month of his death and took to lighting a peace candle with Laura in George's memory for that week in each month – and the migraines disappeared.

Bringing our awareness to the emotional pain gives us the opportunity to find a more loving way of incorporating that experience into our lives. Barbara allowed her tears to flow on her morning walks as she remembered the precious times spent with George. This became her sacred time to reflect and be with her self. As the first anniversary of George's death came closer, Barbara once again experienced a migraine and immediately revisited the rituals she had created and added some other things into her daily life that were meaningful for her and allowed her to express her emotions of sadness.

Often friends and other family members may not be 'available' to hear a person's continuing distress around grieving. That doesn't mean that *we* shouldn't honour our own process and make sure that we find a listening heart to hear our anguish or find rituals or other ways of coming to peace around our feelings.

It is common for people to resist letting their tears fall and yet this is the body's natural release of stored emotion. The endorphins in our tears give us a sense of relaxation and relief once shed. They are the body's own pain relievers and contain potent chemicals that soothe us physically, mentally and emotionally. As we let go our resistance to 'what is' and weep the tears of our distress, they become the pathway to our spirit.

In my family tears were rarely, if ever, shed. For many years I bottled up all my emotions, although I wasn't conscious of doing so. What this meant was that I would 'disappear' from conversations, events or occasions where tears might flow. Such was my fear about crying that I believed that if I started, I might never stop. Once my resistance was worn down through trauma and illness, I wept buckets and then more buckets, then more buckets.

So many people want to hear about the rosy path to healing. How much vitamin C should I take? How long should I meditate? How many juices should I drink? How many people do I need to forgive? They seldom want to know that real healing lies not in the recipe but in the release of long-stored emotions.

Now my eyes mist up easily when people tell me of the anguish in their lives and weeping occurs very rarely. People have sometimes asked me whether I've had to 'harden my heart' in order to hear the tens of thousands of stories people have shared with me over the past 20 years. The answer is a resounding 'no!' It has been my experience that it is healthy and appropriate to be compassionately aware of and able to empathise with those who entrust me with their suffering. Burnout and lack of compassion is the destination of those who barricade their hearts against suffering.

Counselling can be very helpful in giving us a broader perspective of our situation. Sometimes we're so caught up in the grief or trauma that it's difficult for us to know how to deal with the challenges we face. Often we don't know what we think until we hear what we say. When we make time for counselling we are also making time for healing to occur. To seek counselling implies that we're worthy of understanding the situation we're in and finding a way to live more peaceably with what has happened. From the moment we make the appointment, we have begun the healing process. Healing requires awareness and awareness is nothing more than love. Again, it is that state we reach when we say, 'Enough' or 'That's it – something's got to change.' In that moment lies the potential for emotional healing.

Participants on our programs at the Quest for Life Centre have often said that everything began to change for them from the moment they decided to attend a residential program. Once we want peace more than anything, the whole universe will conspire to bring it about. It only takes a willingness to change our perceptions.

We generally don't realise that the healing of our emotional wounds will free us from dragging them around for the rest of our lives. Sometimes, especially with grief, we don't want to be free of the pain because it becomes our way of holding onto the person who's gone. Yet, freeing ourselves of the emotional pain allows us to have a happier relationship with others and ourselves in the certain knowledge that love never dies. Grief doesn't last for a certain period of time; it becomes incorporated into our life.

Likewise, as we grow older and death is upon our own horizon, whatever is unresolved from the past becomes more keenly focused in our awareness. It becomes more difficult to keep our unresolved emotions submerged in our consciousness. It is my belief that many older people disappear into dementia because they have no idea or awareness of either the need or the means by which to bring healing to their past.

We are not our feelings; we have feelings. Our identification with our feelings is one of the main obstacles to a more expansive experience of ourselves. We live in a culture that places little value on feelings and relegates them to a safe expression through art, music, theatre or other creative media. Most of us are taught to keep our feelings firmly under control and only expose those that seem nice, safe and socially acceptable. We're then trained to suppress or repress other feelings – even from ourselves – that might be unpredictable, irrational, outrageous or inappropriate. So we learn that some feelings are good and some are bad.

Through the practice of awareness and meditation we have the capacity to witness our feelings rather than be overwhelmed by them or react from them unconsciously. This separation between self and the experience of emotion is invaluable. It gives us the capacity to choose our response rather than simply to react from the feeling. It gives us the opportunity to decide whether it is useful or appropriate to express the feeling or to simply witness and release it.

A few months before I became ill with leukaemia, which happened while I was in the US, I'd separated from my husband. On returning from America, my two young children went to live with their father and I moved in with my parents so that they could care for me. Their home at that time overlooked Middle Harbour in Sydney. I spent many days lying in bed consumed by despair at my predicament. I was 33 years old and expected to die, leaving my two small children motherless; my brother had recently taken his own life. My despair stemmed from the belief that I had no control over my life and I found it an agony to be both powerless and the cause of further pain for my family.

The valley my bedroom overlooked was the habitat of many large, colourful and raucous birds. One morning, a small bird flew past my window and my mind, captured by curiosity, directed my gaze to it, identified it as 'a sparrow' and then I saw myself returning to despair. It was one of those crystal moments of awareness that enabled me to question the reality of despair. I clearly saw the sequence: enmeshed in despair, captured by curiosity, returned to despair. I contemplated the reality of 'despair' when, in the moments the sparrow afforded me, I entertained 'curiosity' instead. In the moment of curiosity, despair had no reality.

So who is in charge of my experience and what is the reality of despair other than what I give to it? This question led me to the conclusion that it was entirely within my responsibility to dictate my reality; or put another way, my 'response-ability' – my ability to respond rather than simply to react.

In order to respond, our ability to witness our experience is essential. If we don't have this ability then we are at the mercy of whatever feelings pass through us. Increasing our awareness and ability to respond rather than react is the path to liberation from feelings. After all, do we want to feel a helpless victim of our circumstances and the feelings precipitated by them or can we be more than that? Such moments have the potential to change the way we view our lives. Are we going to allow feelings to have dominion over us or can we perceive them differently?

It's the difference between feeling 'I am in despair' or 'I am feeling despair'. This may not seem like a marked distinction but, as we'll discover, it is the pathway to being liberated from the intensity of feelings.

All descriptions of reality are temporary hypotheses.

Buddha

Sometimes the feelings we experience may not even have their source within us. We might find it helpful to think of these feelings as waves of energy that enter us from outside of ourselves. They may flow into our orbit from another person or groups of people, even from a movie or a news item on television. These waves of energy might flow through an entire community or nation. Lynch mobs both from history and from the present, though they may not be so named, are thus impelled to react from these waves of emotions.

The feelings are not the problem – we are not responsible for the origin of every feeling that comes into our orbit. We are only responsible for what we do with the feeling. This attitude of awareness eliminates any guilt or shame about the feelings we experience. Some of the more potent feelings of anger, rage, lust, jealousy or fear might enter our awareness as a wave of energy, and it is liberating indeed to witness them rather than give them free rein over our actions.

It is interesting that many participants in our Quest for Life Centre programs have in recent years spoken of a great sadness, uneasiness or underlying grief that they can't explain or account for – that is, they can't identify any event in their own life that might precipitate such feelings. On exploration, they say they're feeling a deep sense of helplessness, powerlessness and sadness about the planet and what's taking place environmentally, economically, politically and socially. Many feel that we're heading for disaster and are feeling completely powerless to bring about change. Some speak of sadness, helplessness and rage about what's happening to the environment, some about refugees, others about the potential or consequences of war or terrorism. Some of the people have been directly affected by terrorism or war but far, far more have been on the periphery of these events and have still been deeply affected.

Why? Because the beliefs that we see enacted in the world hold values that we know will never bring us peace. And yet, peace is what we say we want. We see our leaders, and therefore ourselves, looking for answers through economic, political and military means. We're questioning these answers because it is patently obvious that they are not bringing us what we say we want – peace and happiness.

> *No problem can be solved from the same consciousness that created it.*
>
> *Albert Einstein*

The problems we face in the world today cannot be solved through politics, economics or military force because *they* are not the source of the problem. The source of the problem is spiritual: our fundamental beliefs about life, its value and meaning.

Our beliefs lie in the realm of our consciousness – our spirit – and beliefs impel our behaviours and actions. It is what we believe about life, ourselves, each other and about God that allows us to perpetrate and perpetuate such behaviours. I have avoided using the word 'God' up until now, as so often our ideas about who and what God is limit our understanding. We need to expand the view that religions hold about God to accommodate our growth in understanding.

The increasing polarisation that is taking place in our society disturbs us deeply because we can feel – literally in our cells – the consequences of such beliefs. We are told that, in God's name, we seek to enforce justice and democracy. Our political leaders seem to claim a direct line to a God that will justify their own beliefs. And with righteousness on side we're asked, 'Are you with us or against us?'

We've constructed a God of our own making that gives us the moral authority to perpetrate our limiting beliefs. There are two fundamental beliefs which, when enacted, create most of the problems we encounter in the world. These beliefs are that we are separate from one another and that we have to compete with one another to survive and be happy because there isn't enough of what we need on the planet to go around. Such beliefs spawn and justify behaviours that include violence against each other and destruction of our environment.

Yet, we crave union and yearn for its experience. We are not separate from one another; we are intrinsically empowered by the same life force, and that life force *is* consciousness. What we do to others, through our beliefs, we do to ourselves.

A willingness to question our beliefs and the behaviours that stem from them is the first step in creating peace in our lives. Our feelings are the gateway to understanding the beliefs we hold and the behaviours they generate.

In addition to the feelings we're exposed to from outside of ourselves, we have stored feelings laid down in the tissues of our bodies from traumatic experiences from the past. So we *physically and emotionally* react in the present to the chemical memories laid down in the past, this process being triggered by some similar experience now. The knowledge of this, though now verified and understood, is as yet not incorporated into the way we treat people medically.

Ray grew up in a household where his father drank to excess and had violent outbursts, often involving the physical abuse of his mother. As a young child he recalled often crying himself to sleep because he felt so powerless to stop the violence against his mother. Sometimes he'd feign stomach pains so that he could spend the day at home with his mother, enjoying her company in the calm of his father's absence. Ray was also aware that his mother often reached for her 'little green pills' that somehow made her life more tolerable.

As he grew into his pre-teen years, he felt ashamed that his cowardice had stopped him from intervening and protecting his mother from his father. As a teenager, Ray fluctuated between being angry at his mother for neither leaving nor standing up for herself and being angry and disappointed with himself for his perceived cowardice in not defending her. He never spoke directly of how he felt, but his behaviour throughout his teen years was ample evidence of his deep distress.

Ray set off early in life to make something of himself and to prove that he was worthy of respect. He admitted that he was proving it as much to himself as to anyone else. His father had repeated over and over to him that 'the mark of a man is his ability to work'. He married his childhood sweetheart before he was 20 and while he never abused her physically and, indeed, their life together seemed ideal, Ray was often away on business, leaving Marion to raise their children and attend to most of the day-to-day concerns of family life. Ray took the outward trappings of the private education he provided for his children, holidays, the house, cars and lifestyle to be sufficient indication of both his success and his love for his family.

There were no arguments in their marriage except for the occasional ones when Marion requested that Ray spend more time with her and the children. He would quickly retaliate with, 'You're more than happy with the lifestyle I provide and that doesn't come out of thin air, you know!' or words to that effect – and that would be the end of the discussion.

In time, their three children left home to pursue careers and lives of their own. One day not long after the youngest had left and Ray was soon to retire, Marion told him that she was going away to do something meaningful in her own life. It wasn't that she didn't love him, though she wasn't entirely sure anymore that she did, she said. She simply wanted to find out who she was, what she wanted and what had meaning for her. Marion had never worked and wanted her freedom to do so now that she didn't have to care for a family – she'd joked in the past that Ray was like her fourth child but at least he was absent a good deal of the time.

Ray was inwardly distraught but accepted her decision without rancour, argument or bitterness. He loved Marion and found it easy to blame himself for his long absences that had left her lonely and unfulfilled. After all, blaming himself was a familiar pattern.

Ray waited patiently for Marion's return. He felt he was in limbo as she explored a world without him. She would telephone him quite frequently to let him know of her movements and what she was doing. And while he drew comfort from the fact that she wanted to share with him the stories of her life, each time he asked when she was coming back, she'd shrug him off with a noncommittal answer.

Ray developed a stomach ulcer within six months of Marion's absence and told friends that it was because he missed her cooking. Months turned into two years and all the while Ray waited. Sleep had become elusive for him and he started having panic attacks when he closed his eyes at night, as well as occasionally during the day. He'd always sworn he'd never use drugs and alcohol, given the effects he'd seen these have in his childhood, yet here he was now dependent on drugs for his ulcer, for sleeping, depression and anxiety. It was the desire to be free of medication that impelled him to seek help.

Ray realised that he was feeling once more like the powerless little boy of his childhood. Again, a woman was the cause of his helplessness. Again, he felt he could do nothing to change or stop what was happening or persuade her to act differently. He was paralysed by fear and powerlessness.

Ray wept as he remembered the helplessness of the child who couldn't protect his mother and he accepted the reassurance that it wasn't that little boy's fault. As this recognition became conscious, Ray found healing for the childhood memories stored within. This enabled him to no longer react as the child but respond like a man instead. No longer the helpless victim of his history, he was able to respond with clear boundaries about what was appropriate for him now, and what he would no longer tolerate.

If Marion needed her freedom, so be it. He would move on in his own life rather than wait for her to decide his fate. He discovered respect for himself and felt it would be best to honour both of them by *him* being decisive about their future. As this healing took place, Ray's panic attacks disappeared and his sleep once more became sound and refreshing. His stomach ulcer subsided and healed almost as quickly. Interestingly, even though she was now living interstate, Marion 'felt' the change in Ray before he was able to share it with her.

When we bring our awareness to embedded feelings of the past, we bring with it the healing touch of love and compassion. Awareness *is* love. In that moment we are transformed and the ripples of transformation flow into every corner of our lives to bring healing. For people connected in love, these transformations can be detected long before a person speaks or acts. Their presence feels different. This has nothing to do with being physically in a person's presence, as distance plays no part in the energy of love. When we transform a pattern and release it from ourselves, the consequent ripples flow without impediment.

Marion returned to live with Ray soon after and their relationship became closer than it had ever been. They had created enough love in their relationship to allow for the healing of ancient wounds. If Marion hadn't left, Ray would not have found the buried wound that still affected how he lived in the present. In leaving Ray, she'd provided him with the opportunity to confront, understand and release himself from the wounded pattern he'd formed in childhood. Sometimes, when everything feels like it's falling apart, it's actually falling together.

The wound that Ray lived with up until its healing had had a profound effect upon his life. He saw how it had influenced his choice of career (he refused to employ anyone because he didn't want to deal with staff and risk feeling 'out of control'); his choice of partner (Marion knew of his childhood but there was an unsaid agreement that they'd never mention it – and she loved him); the way he raised his children (by being mostly absent for fear of either not being enough for them or too much for them); his persistent admonishments to them about drugs and alcohol in their teen years (which precluded conversation and lead them to sneak alcohol or smoke marijuana – unbeknownst to him) and in a million other ways.

Ray saw that his quick retaliation over the years to Marion's request for more of his company was simply the emotional bandaid he kept over the wound of his childhood. It is a characteristic of healing that when we bring awareness – that is, love – to a long-held pattern, many other unseen wounds are also healed instantly. The ramifications of this healing are profound – the consequences extend from changing our biology to one more conducive to health and healing, to changing our interactions with people and circumstances. We are no longer the person we were but have become transformed through our willingness to bring love, compassion and understanding to our emotional wounds.

Many adults were taught in their childhood not to feel any emotion too strongly and certainly not to talk about so-called negative feelings – hurt, anger, despair, fear, depression or sadness. We may have been taught that even the positive emotions of love, happiness and joy must be kept within controlled bounds. These lessons in suppressing our feelings were generally never given to us consciously. They were conveyed subtly, and not so subtly, by comments like, 'You shouldn't feel like that', 'There's no reason to feel that way', 'Don't get so excited' and of course a very common one, 'Big girls / boys don't cry'.

The journey into our emotional world can feel terrifying to some. Many people, including myself, have described it to be like 'stepping off the edge of the abyss'. This leads many of us to excel in the mental aspects of our lives so that we can ignore or repress our feelings, which in turn leads to a numbing of emotions and a state in which we have neither highs nor lows but live in an emotional wasteland. These people choose to control the unpredictability of their feelings by busying themselves with thinking and achieving. When you ask people who deny their emotional world how they feel about a certain subject, they will invariably tell you what they think about it instead. They may not even have an emotional language to use if their entire family only ever talked about ideas, concepts, beliefs and attitudes rather than feelings.

As we explored in previous chapters, feelings establish themselves in our body via chemicals, hormones and neural pathways long before thoughts, thinking, beliefs and reasoning play their part. We are feeling beings before we are thinking ones. Our thoughts and beliefs may modify, justify, explain or enhance our feelings, but the feelings were there first. Thoughts are connected to our conscious mind and will, and feelings belong to a less rational and primal place within us. This is why we sometimes can't identify what it is that we're feeling; we know we're feeling something yet we can't find the words to accurately identify it. I think of these as the 'pre-three' feelings – those that were laid down in our biology before we had a language to articulate or understand them.

In later life, we can be precipitated into the experience of these 'pre-three' feelings and yet are unable to find the words to describe them. Through awareness and compassion we can accept and embrace this part of ourselves which is emotionally immature. This compassion for our own wounded self leads to compassion for others; the level to which we're willing to embrace our own sadness, rage, loss, despair, grief, anguish, pain, fear, terror, abandonment, loneliness or whatever emotion it might be, is the level to which we can be a companion for those who likewise are experiencing these same emotions. We may not know exactly how another person feels yet we know how that emotion feels for us and, having embraced it, no longer fear it.

This ability to not judge our feelings but accept, witness or embrace them instead is the pathway to liberation, where we discover a beauty in our sadness and in our joy. Such emotions carve themselves deeply into our being and enable us to feel the fullness of life. If we don't allow our feelings to move through us because we resist, suppress or judge them, then they remain blocked and stored in our bodies. This has consequences in each aspect of ourselves – physically, mentally, emotionally and spiritually. Lack of awareness about, judgement of, or fear of feelings is implicated in all illnesses, however they manifest themselves.

We may be afraid to feel the fear, grief, sadness or whatever, and therein lies the problem! We need to find effective ways of witnessing our feelings without becoming stuck or overwhelmed by them. Accepting our emotions allows us to feel and release them; judging them, denying them, running away from them or suppressing them blocks the free flow of energy and leads to consequences in our health. Fear and anger are often entwined and those who come close to our fear may well be repelled by our anger. By being willing to explore our anger and uncover its root we can bring healing to our fear and find peace and wisdom in its wake.

At the other end of the spectrum are people who find their feelings are constantly dictating their reality and who have minimal control over their emotional equilibrium. They live with seesawing emotions and have little ability to witness what they're feeling because they are so consumed by the experience of each feeling. Each emotion feels all-consuming and hyper-real for them, so that they are like a helpless cork bobbing on an emotional ocean of feelings beyond their control. Finding the part of us that can 'parent' the feeling-consumed child within can be a helpful starting point when emotions dictate our reality.

Anger

Some people get stuck in one emotion and constantly react from that place. Fear and anger are two such feelings that people can give their whole life over to, constantly reacting from those emotional states. The person who specialises in anger may well have found that it was the only way to get their needs met as a child. Anger and bluster are very effective tools for intimidating others – especially those who live in a state of fear!

Anger is not a 'bad' emotion. Healthily expressed anger discharges disharmony from within ourselves. An unhealthy or inappropriate expression of anger is when we use it as a means to wound other people or ourselves. Wherever there is anger – in ourselves, in others, in our community, in our nation – we can choose to see it as a call for help or healing rather than as an attack.

An understanding of anger can help us become less fearful of it and more able to cope in its presence. Anger is also healthy when it is the enabling force that helps us set clear boundaries, to speak our truth or to reclaim our power when we've habitually given it away to other people or situations. Any strong feeling is an energy that needs to move, that needs to be discharged or expressed.

It is helpful to realise that we're rarely upset for the reasons we think. Below the surface of our anger may well fester a range of beliefs, unmet needs or feelings that we haven't yet made conscious.

This realisation gives us a better perspective from which to respond to anger rather than simply to react from it. A friend of mine, Lyn Perkin, often co-facilitates with me on our residential Quest for Life Centre programs. Lyn uses the following diagram to assist participants in understanding anger more effectively.

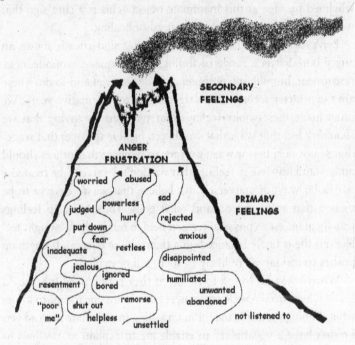

SECONDARY FEELINGS

ANGER FRUSTRATION

PRIMARY FEELINGS

worried   abused

judged   powerless   sad

hurt   rejected

put down

fear   anxious

inadequate   restless

disappointed

jealous

ignored   humiliated

resentment   bored   unwanted

abandoned

"poor me"   shut out   remorse

helpless   not listened to

unsettled

Language of the wounded self

I can't . . .	but . . .
I have to . . .	if only . . .
I should . . .	never . . .
I ought . . .	always . . .
try . . .	impossible . . .

Have you ever reacted in a way that is out of all proportion to the stimulus of your anger? Suddenly we have an outburst over something that we're barely aware of as an issue. 'Outburst' is an excellent word to describe precisely what happens. It's like a vent goes down into a volcano and out bursts a reaction out of all proportion to the stimulus. It can even be over something as trivial as a dresser drawer getting stuck and KAPOW!, we're suddenly overwhelmed by rage at this inanimate object. This is a sure sign that we have an emotional backlog in need of healing.

Lyn's diagram illustrates that festering underneath many an angry outburst is a range of feelings – inadequacy, woundedness, resentment, humiliation, impotence, sadness, grief and so on. These are the primary feelings that originated in our formative years. We often judge these sooky feelings that we resist by saying that we *shouldn't* feel that way; that we should be able to cope; that something's not fair; that it wasn't meant to happen; that others should understand how we're feeling; that we don't deserve to be treated a particular way; or conversely, we believe that we *do* deserve to be treated that way, and on and on it goes. These pent-up feelings usually manifest as physical tension held in our body. We might feel like our life is finely balanced on a tightrope of tension. If anything pushes us too far we're likely to snap, fall or explode.

When I was ill, I used to think, 'If they really loved me, they'd know what I need!' Such arrogance! How is anyone meant to know what is going on inside me if I'm unwilling to articulate it? And yet, I didn't have a vocabulary to enable me to explain my feelings to myself, let alone to other people. It can be a comfort to those who love someone with a life-threatening illness or who are living with any significant challenge to know that we'll probably get it wrong most of the time when we offer help! For instance, if you get someone a chair he's likely to think, 'I can get my own chair'. If you don't get him a chair he's as likely to think, 'Why don't you get me a chair? Don't you know I'm sick?' The sooner we surrender to not trying to get it right, the better.

Because many of us don't have a language to accurately describe our emotional wounds or we are judgemental of them, our feelings become a hodge-podge of pent-up energy seeking an outlet. These feelings build up, just like in that volcano, and we explode with the secondary feelings of frustration and anger. The primary feelings of being hurt, sad, powerless, inadequate and helpless give impetus, energy and fuel to the secondary feelings of frustration and anger. Perhaps we don't want to admit to our vulnerabilities – the feelings of being hurt, sad, rejected, shut out, humiliated, resentful and so on – and use anger as a way of warding off intruders, even ourselves, from our sacred wounded territory. Anger and frustration usually make us feel more powerful than accessing and embracing our vulnerability.

Once we release ourselves from the accumulated anger through the healing of our emotions, we discover an emotional equilibrium that allows us to be wholly present to each moment without any need to *react* to it. Instead, we respond moment by moment in our life from a place of peace, compassion and inner contentment. When a situation arises in which we feel anger, then it is only in response to *this* moment rather than the historical anger stored in our body of experience.

For instance, say my partner makes a commitment on my behalf. I might feel angry that she / he hasn't consulted me. I might well say, 'I notice that you've made a commitment on my behalf. I imagine you thought I wouldn't mind. However, I feel angry that you committed me to something without asking me first.' This embodies only this occasion rather than being delivered with an unresolved load of anger from past experiences.

If there *is* an emotional backlog of me feeling like my partner has no respect for my boundaries, then I'm more likely to react from the stored feelings of resentment and say something along the lines of, 'You never listen to me and you're always living my life for me.' This is unlikely to lead to a constructive interchange. Staying up to date in our relationships, both with ourselves and other people, is a healthy foundation for peace.

There are some people in our lives that we need to consciously resolve issues with and other people who activate in us a need to resolve our *inner* issues. This may well happen without their knowledge or participation, as in the case of Ray and Marion. Ray didn't need to resolve his issues of powerlessness with Marion. The situation with Marion, however, enabled him to confront, understand and resolve the issue of his childhood wounds. This was enough for him to leave behind his childish reactions and to respond like a mature man instead.

Feelings are just feelings. Let yourself have the full gamut of them. You are not crazy, bad or wrong to feel the way you do. What matters is what you *do* with the feelings. We all have a capacity to choose our thoughts but the only choice we have with feelings is how we're going to handle them.

Judy's baby, Jason, died three weeks after his slightly premature birth. The circumstances surrounding Jason's birth and death were already difficult for Judy because her mother was in the last months of her life and her partner, Tony, was overseas for a major sporting event.

Judy's mother had been holding on for the birth of her first grandson but with his unexpected death, her will to live evaporated and she followed him within a week. By the time Tony returned a few days later, both his baby son and his mother-in-law had been buried.

Judy had galvanised herself to cope with both losses as well as arranging her son's and mother's funerals. She was used to coping on her own because of Tony's gruelling training sessions and his frequent absences, but she found the grief unbearable.

Tony returned with a mixture of disbelief, guilt about his absence, and shock and devastation that he'd lost his son and Judy's mother. His feelings overshadowed any pride in his considerable sporting achievements.

Their relationship deteriorated rapidly as Judy and Tony, both caught up in guilt, self-blame, recriminations, grief, rage, profound sadness, powerlessness and confusion, began to see each other as the cause – rather than the events that had precipitated such powerful emotions – of their distress.

They separated and Judy's grief continued to undermine her peace. Caught up in the cycle of guilt and blame, she believed that 'there are some things beyond healing'. And the fact is, if we believe we're beyond healing then there's very little anyone else can do about it.

We sometimes feel that making peace with some dreadful thing that has happened in our life means that we're saying that it was all right for that thing to have happened. That's not the case, but we may feel that the only way to continue with our life is to hold onto the unresolved feelings engendered by the experience. Holding onto such feelings keeps the person who's gone present in our lives. We may feel that to let go of the grief, angst and upset is to let go of the person and yet, it is precisely these feelings that inhibit our ability to connect lovingly with the non-physical presence of our loved one in the certain knowledge that love or consciousness never dies.

Protecting the Wounded Self

We continue to gather beliefs, ideas and attitudes to protect us from confronting our unhealed emotional wounds of the past for just as long as we need to. These beliefs are valuable to us and can provide an effective strategy to deal with our vulnerability. However, consciously choosing to maintain those beliefs for the reason of protection is very different to unconsciously reacting to life from them.

For Judy, knowing she can *choose* not to go with a friend to the pre-school because she feels too emotionally vulnerable is different to unconsciously avoiding anything to do with children henceforth.

There are basically three ways of dealing with our emotions. We can *deny* they exist, which takes energy to keep them from being shown either to ourselves or other people. We can *indulge* them and immerse ourselves in them – either splattering our emotions around freely, perhaps with the excuse, 'It's just the way I am!' or imploding and becoming moody, sulky and emotionally unavailable to other people. Or we can **consciously acknowledge** our emotions. Then we can either witness them or give them expression in a way that doesn't wound others or ourselves.

If we're upset about someone's behaviour we can pretend that everything's fine – and the upset quietly festers underneath. This **denial** often then looks for further ammunition to support our view; we then build up further resentment about the person, or the situation, and can move either to gossiping behind their back or exploding at them or someone else – perhaps completely unrelated to the source of our angst – perhaps even yelling at them, throwing something or hitting them. This is simply an indulgence of our emotions – acting out our inner distress in the most unskilful of ways and creating more baggage for the future. Or, put another way, we perpetuate the past thus securing our future.

In the third course of action that lies open to us – acknowledging to ourselves with awareness that we're feeling upset – we take responsibility for the upset. Not for its origin but for how we're going to handle it. We allow ourselves to feel upset and see whether it has a relationship to one or more of our habitual patterns. Having explored the feeling, we choose whether it is appropriate or helpful to ourselves or to the other person to let them know how we're feeling. Sometimes it will be appropriate and helpful; at other times the feeling won't be about the other person at all but one of our familiar patterns from the past. We become more aware so that we might release ourselves from its habitual reaction.

Mansion of Emotion

You might find the image opposite a helpful one as you begin to identify and witness your emotional world. Imagine that within your mind you have a mansion with as many rooms as you have feelings. There is the 'fear room', the 'sad room', and rooms for not coping, happiness, joy, despair, depression, panic and so on. You might find it helpful to draw your own set of rooms as in the illustration below.

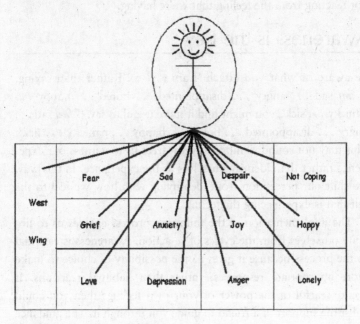

Fear	Sad	Despair	Not Coping
Grief	Anxiety	Joy	Happy
Love	Depression	Anger	Lonely

West Wing

Mansion of Emotion

We are not responsible for having the feeling.
We are responsible for what we *do* with the feeling.

The Process of Witnessing our Feelings

1. 'This is how it feels to be me feeling this feeling.'
2. 'It's all right for me to feel this feeling.'
3. 'This is how this feeling feels for me – aware of what happens in my body and my mind. Not acting out of this feeling but feeling it with awareness.'

Fill in your illustration with the 'rooms' you identify in your own inner mansion of emotions. This practice of awareness gives us the capacity to witness ourselves *experiencing* the emotion rather than identifying ourselves *as* the emotion. This is the first step in not reacting from the feeling that we're having.

Awareness is the Key

Be aware of what you attach 'I am . . .' to. Rather than saying, 'I *am* sad . . . angry . . . disappointed . . . bored . . . happy . . . panicky . . . sick', you might find it more useful to say, 'I *feel* sad . . . angry . . . disappointed . . . bored . . . happy . . . panicky . . . sick'. This may not sound significant, yet it frees us to witness our experience rather than identify ourselves as the experience. In this way, we shift our perception from identifying with how we feel to the self that is experiencing the feeling.

The implementation of the following process enables us to liberate ourselves from the cycles of re-action. Awareness is essential to the process because it gives us the possibility of choice to make more appropriate responses, rather than habitual reactions. If you're fearful of the power of your own feelings then you could enlist the support of a friend to guide you through it. The guidance of a counsellor may be very helpful if you're deeply afraid of what you might experience. Choose someone familiar with meditation and the witnessing of emotions. Another approach is to set yourself a time limit for exploring a particular 'room'. You may also find it helpful to begin with your less confronting feelings.

There are three steps to this process. The **first** is to identify the feeling that you're having. Sometimes this can be a challenge, as it can be a hodge-podge or smorgasbord of feelings. For example, it might be a combination of shock, disbelief, confusion and fear; or perhaps it is a feeling we cannot name because it is one of the 'pre-three' feelings I mentioned earlier. If it's a composite feeling then just give it a name to be known by – 'the dreads', 'impending doom', 'helpless and hopeless'. So then the process goes like this: 'This is how it feels to be me [in this case we'll use 'Petrea'] feeling the dreads' or 'This is how it feels to be Petrea feeling sad' or 'This is how it feels to be Petrea feeling despair' or 'This is how it feels to be Petrea feeling impending doom' – one of my all-time favourites!

The **second** step is to give yourself permission to feel this way: 'It's okay to feel this sadness . . . grief . . . despair . . . dread . . . fear . . . impending doom' or whatever the feeling might be.

This is the tricky step because most of us don't want to feel the feeling but it's our very resistance to feeling the feeling that is the problem. We're afraid to feel the fear because we might tumble into the abyss of whatever it is that we're resisting. It is our fear of the feeling that stops us from exploring it! When we take the light of our consciousness – and perhaps the company of another person such as a counsellor, friend, support group – into the darkness of our 'fear room', paradoxically, we begin to lose our terror.

The **third** step is simply to feel the feeling with awareness. 'This is how it feels to be Petrea feeling despair . . . sadness . . . impending doom' and so on. Even though this part of the practice might involve crying or feeling the physical sensations of fear or rage or panic, we continue to witness the experience rather than allow ourselves to be consumed by it or react from it; a sense of 'yes, I can feel the sick feeling of fear in my stomach. I can feel the tightening of my chest, the prickly sensation up my neck. Yes, this is how it feels to be Petrea feeling fear.'

I know that describing the process this way makes it sound easier to do than it sometimes is; however, it actually does become easier when we gently bring our awareness to our emotional wounds. Gradually we're able to throw open all the doors in our inner mansion of emotion and move freely and peaceably in and out of each room without feeling that we *are* that room. There's a very real difference between the experience of 'I am feeling fear; it's okay to feel fear; and this is how fear feels for me,' than, 'I am terrified.'

If we apply this process to the feeling of 'not coping' we see how helpful it can become.

Step one 'This is how it feels to be Petrea not coping.'

Step two 'It's okay not to cope.' (Who said you have to cope all the time?)

Step three 'This is how not coping feels for me.'

The third step might involve pulling the doona over our head; maybe allowing ourselves to have a good weep or scream (perhaps in the car with the windows wound up and the music up loud if you're worried about the neighbours' or family's reactions); going for a long walk; cancelling commitments by saying something like, 'Count me out today until 2 pm, I won't be coping until then. Come 2 pm, I'll have a shower, put on a face and go do my life again, but count me out until 2!'

We can be so fearful of not coping that we suppress all our feelings in case they lead us into feeling out of control. We might do this by endlessly procrastinating, keeping ourselves overly busy, compulsive behaviours or an increase in our drug of choice. Allowing ourselves the time to not cope, paradoxically, becomes a way of coping. It is the fear of not coping that is the problem. When we find more skilful ways of being with the feeling of not coping, we begin to lose our fear of it.

Children take to the diagram of the Mansion of Emotion very well. It gives them a sense that it's okay to have those feelings, that they're perfectly normal and that what matters is becoming aware of their feelings and expressing them appropriately. As children, we all needed to hear reflected back to us from our parents, teachers and others how we were feeling and a validation that it was understandable and okay for us to feel that way. That's how we learned a language to describe our feelings.

For many of us this didn't happen however, and we learned to either suppress or deny our feelings, or only express them in unhealthy or ineffective ways. We needed to have someone empathise with us when we were children so we could learn that we are allowed to have our emotional experiences. It's never too late to learn though, and we can find healthier ways of acknowledging and expressing our feelings by helping our children to do the same: 'I can see that you're feeling very sad and upset.' 'Your body language tells me you're feeling frustrated and grumpy about this. Is that right?' 'I imagine that could be quite a scary experience for you. Tell me about it.'

The emotional wounds gathered in our childhood remain stored within us until we acknowledge and release them. If we're fearful of our feelings then we may well have stored baggage in the rooms of our Mansion of Emotion. Once we acknowledge, witness or express these feelings, we find the emotional need that wasn't met by our parents or other adults in our early life.

No matter how wonderfully we were parented, almost every child emerges into adulthood with some emotional healing work to be completed. Once we're emotionally up to date with our lives we'll need skills to identify, release or express our current feelings so that we don't store a backlog of emotionally blocked energy. Finding ways of expressing our needs can be a challenge to us. Yet it is essential if we're to mature into people who can give and receive love.

The West Wing – Communication

Emotionally mature people take responsibility for, and become a committed parent to, their inner wounded self. The question can then become, 'How will I parent this part of me that is feeling wounded?'

rather than expecting the world to change or to guess what we need. Instead we ask: 'How can I provide that for myself?'

In some families, or within ourselves, there may be a whole 'west wing' of the mansion – the extension on the house that we don't talk about, where we must not venture. This might stem from a family secret, a painful incident from the past, our worst nightmare unfolding around us or a subject considered taboo by our family. There may be padlocks and bolts on the door to the west wing and a ferocious dog to guard its entrance! Members of our family may put out subtle but unmistakeable barriers to conversations that venture anywhere near matters of the west wing.

Needless to say, the energy locked up in the west wing drains us and denies us peace. Perhaps there was sexual or physical abuse in our history and conversations that venture near it are stifled, ignored, trivialised or are beyond articulation. This is when we need to be aware of placing our 'pearls', our vulnerabilities, before swine.

The emotional wounds that caused us such anguish become our pearls – the means by which we get to know and understand ourselves so deeply. It takes courage to heal such wounds but, then, what is our choice? If we want peace more than we want to hold onto the anguish, more than we want to blame our history and use it as an excuse for who we are now, more than we want to be right or exercise righteous indignation, then we must bring the healing touch of our awareness to these emotional wounds.

We are often not aware of the west wing within ourselves. We simply cannot see the emotional patterns of the past that affect our daily lives until we take notice of it. Once we realise that we have a painful part of ourselves locked up, we can gently bring our awareness to heal us of our past wounds. For me, creating so much pain for my children and parents through dying was my west wing. I maintained a very 'positive' exterior in order not to acknowledge the possibility of my death.

Once I realised this, I was able to bring the concept of death and the feelings embedded in it to the surface and witness and express the feelings trapped within. However, I did not choose to do this at 3 am when our minds have a tendency to catastrophise everything. This liberated me to then have long-overdue conversations with family members, get my will and funeral in order and to write letters and make tapes for my children for the future. It loosened the bonds around uttering the words, 'I love you' to those I treasured in my life. After all, why was I saving those words for a rainy day? Now I tell those I treasure in my life that I love them on a daily basis!

The formula of 'I notice . . .' 'I imagine . . .' 'I feel . . .' explained below, can be a very useful one for dealing with challenging conversations. When we use this formula – perhaps not with the exact words – we're endeavouring **firstly,** to describe the behaviour or the situation that we see is happening. **Secondly,** we're endeavouring to compassionately understand how it might be for the other person, and **thirdly,** we're letting the person know how we're feeling about the situation. This formula conveys that the other person is not the problem. It's as if we stand hand-in-hand together looking at the problem rather than seeing each other as the problem. Here are some examples of how this formula might be used:

> 'I notice that your room is a mess and I've asked you three times this week to clean it up.' (Perhaps this is better directed at your children rather than your partner!)

> 'I imagine it is not a priority for you, however it is for me.'

> 'I feel angry and upset that what I've asked you to do hasn't been done. Can we talk about this, please?'

This approach is very different from screaming at the kids and telling them how hopeless and feral they are, and can work well on the really difficult conversations that we often avoid such as:

Example 1

'I notice that whenever I want to talk to you about what happened to me when I was a child you change the subject . . . walk out of the room . . . go to the fridge . . . tell me not to be silly . . . tell me it's all past history' . . . or whatever the behaviour is.

'I imagine you don't want to talk about it because it's in the past . . . it's a painful subject . . . you think I'm blaming you . . .' or whatever you feel compassionately might be the root cause of their dismissal.

'I feel sad . . . alone . . . humiliated . . . angry . . . estranged from you . . . because we don't seem able to communicate about this subject. Can we please talk about it together?'

Example 2

'I notice that whenever I want to talk to you about driving more slowly you become angry . . . speed up . . . go quiet . . . get moody . . . laugh it off.

'I imagine that driving fast is something you enjoy or you don't realise that you're speeding . . . that it's just the way you drive.

'I feel really frightened when you drive that way and I'm wondering how we can talk about it together.'

Example 3

'I notice that when I try to talk to you about the fact that I might die from this disease you change the subject . . . try and cheer me up . . . tell me to be positive . . . tell me I've got colour in my cheeks . . . pour a Scotch . . . stop me.

'I imagine that you might be as frightened of the future as I am . . . might find it as difficult as I do . . . are as sad about the possibility as I am . . . it might be your worst nightmare too . . . you don't have words for it either.

'I'm feeling more and more alone with my thoughts because you only seem able to hear the "positive" or cheerful parts of me and I need to talk to you because you're my best friend . . . I'm sad and lost and want to share my thoughts with you . . . I'm isolated by my fears and need to talk them through with you . . . I can't make arrangements and let you know what I want in the future and I feel anxious about that.'

Example 4

'I notice that when I've mentioned your driving in the past nothing changes . . . you become angry . . . you laugh at me and tell me I'm a scaredy cat . . . you ignore me.

'I imagine that my thoughts and feelings on the subject are of little interest to you . . . an aggravation for you . . . of no consequence to you.

'I feel angry and upset that you ignore my pleas for you to drive more slowly and I'm letting you know that I'll be making other arrangements to arrive at the destination . . . I won't travel with you in the future . . . I'll be driving from here on in.'

Sometimes this simple formula is best presented in the form of a letter. If the subject that you want to discuss is considered a thorny one and conversation about it seems impossible, then putting it in writing can have real benefits – it enables the other person to read your thoughts and react to them privately; they can throw the letter on the floor, re-read it and weep, ignore it or mull over it and come back to you later for a discussion.

Sometimes it is enough to have conveyed the information about how you feel and things begin to change automatically. And some-times it's not even about the other person at all but communicating the feelings fulfils our need to understand and heal our emotional self. Don't expect a response from the other person. If they choose to ignore what you've written, then you know more about that person and their ability to respond. Their response might equally come in the form of a hug, a gesture, a kiss on the cheek or a flower on your pillow.

The important part is that you have fulfilled your responsibility, which is to acknowledge and express yourself in a way that was never intended to wound – your intention is very important. If there is any intention to wound the other person, there will be a hidden barb in your words. Make sure your intention is honourable and that it is an honest communication based on the need to share your thoughts and feelings.

Writing Letters

Expressing ourselves in a really poisonous letter can sometimes be very therapeutic. Instead of judging our emotions, we let them flow. But this version of the letter is unlikely to bring about reconciliation and will be better burnt or binned at its completion! We all know how unhelpful it is to have someone say to us, 'You shouldn't feel that way', so don't do it to yourself.

Writing letters can help us access our emotions and express them in a healthy way. We can even write to people who are no longer in our lives, who have died or who we are divorced from! The healing is in the bringing to consciousness of your feelings in an appropri-ate and manageable way and getting the energy of the feelings moving. Again, this letter might be better unread by anyone but us.

Writing to our children – regardless of their age – can be a tremendously healing and helpful thing to do. So often we get caught up in the behaviour of our children rather than connecting with the 'being' beyond the behaviour. Our conversations can deteriorate to a litany of corrections about behaviour rather than focusing on loving the 'being' regardless of the behaviour – easier said than done sometimes! We can still use the same formula, though feel free to adjust the wording according to the situation. We might, for instance, want to write a letter that affirms what is special in our child – what are the gifts that he or she has brought to the planet? Is he athletic? Is she a good team player? Is he compassionate and kind to people or animals? Does she have good powers of concentration? Is he quick-witted or dexterous? Does she have the ability to bring joy, laughter and happiness to others? Is he considerate of other people's feelings or viewpoints – or whatever it is that we see is special in our child.

We might imagine how it feels for our child to have grown up in the particular circumstances of our family. Was it challenging, fun, traumatic, different from what we all expected? What might their perspective be and what were the strengths, idiosyncrasies and gifts that we saw them bring to the family?

Then we can let them know how we feel about who they are and what they'll be able to accomplish in the world, or thank them for the gift that they are to us. I know of many young people who keep these letters in their wallets or somewhere special for years, and they've told me what strength and comfort their parents' words have been to them.

If we have a young person who's engaging in risky behaviour, then affirming the faith we have in them can be a guiding light or a lifeline to them and a comfort to us. Living in a state of fearful expectation is an agony and accomplishes little except destroying our peace of mind as well.

The following practice might sound a bit twee or simple yet it has the power to transform lives – both ours and the person we're intending to uplift, support or encourage. This practice can be used with people who we have problems communicating with, who appear stuck in a reactive or emotional state, are 'difficult', or present a challenge in our life. It's simple to do and brings us a sense of control and the possibility of healing – we simply send them a rainbow.

I began a similar practice to the following one with my children when I was separated from them during my illness. To this day, more than 20 years on, my children and I rarely have a conversation or email that doesn't include the words, 'I'm sending you rainbows' or 'I'm under the other end of the rainbow', or something similar.

Sending Rainbows

Choose a quiet time of the day – or any time the person comes into our awareness, for that matter! It might be during the quiet time that we devote to ourselves each day or we can do it if we find ourselves fretting about this person. We can send rainbows to places, people and situations, regardless of distance. As one participant on a Quest for Life Centre program said, 'Love can bridge all distances. Surely the substance of rainbows is love.'

To send a rainbow, bring yourself into the present by connecting with the senses of your body. Be aware of your weight and posture, the pressure of your clothing and the air against your skin. Be aware of all the sounds around you, within and outside the space you're in. Focus for a moment or two on your breathing, being aware of each inward and outward breath. Feel the rising and falling of your abdomen or notice the expansion and contraction of your rib cage with each breath. Allow yourself to relax more deeply with each breath.

Imagine that you're under one end of a rainbow, that comes right down through the ceiling and surrounds and envelops you in its light and colour. Imagine it flowing through your body into mother Earth beneath your feet. Breathe in the light and colours of the rainbow; a soft iridescent mist of light and colour that flows inward with each breath. Breathing in all the colours of the rainbow, imagine them gathering in your heart. Bless them with your love and extend the other end of the rainbow out through the ceiling to the person you want to uplift, encourage, support or forgive.

Imagine this person bathed in the light and colour of the rainbow, filled with its peace and magic. See them in their magnificence – rather than in their illness, fear, depression, anxiety or their particular behaviour. See the beauty of their being strengthened, uplifted and made whole by the light and colours of the rainbow. Extend your love and blessings across the rainbow to them, bringing them peace and strength – connected to you through the power of love, as if you see them blossoming into all that they are in their essence. In this way you call forth and empower the goodness and strength in them rather than seeing them in their weakness or whatever state you might previously have labelled them. Spend a minute or two holding the image of them as whole, healed, at peace, radiant, immersed in love.

If you're using this practice as a means of forgiving someone, a situation or a group of people, you may find that your rainbow will not yet stretch all the way. Just like a rainbow in nature, it might seem to go only part of the way. Let it be; you are laying down the energetic pathway for a different kind of relationship with that person or situation; it is another way of letting go of the habitual reactions while endeavouring to create a new way of relating to one another.

It can be helpful to have someone talk you through this rainbow practice. Using it for self-forgiveness or forgiveness of others is detailed in a longer version on my *Gift of Forgiveness* CD. If you're using the rainbow practice for self-healing or to extend healing and support to others, then you will find that version on my *Rainbows to Heal* CD.

People often want to fast-forward to forgiveness without acknowledging or feeling some of the uncomfortable emotions that might be stored around a particular event or person. We cannot access the view from the mountaintop of forgiveness without travelling through the valley to its destination. This journey through understanding, compassion and acceptance is often laced with emotion, yet the willingness to make the journey enables us to arrive at forgiveness quite naturally and without a sense of repressing or overlooking emotions. We may need to cry, remonstrate, write or talk about whatever happened to us until we arrive at that place of acceptance, understanding and wisdom.

The process of forgiveness might or might not involve communicating with the person involved. Each situation is different and there are no right answers, only the ones that *feel* right for us. It may be appropriate to find a path to forgiveness solely within ourselves. It may be equally of value to find a way of expressing to the person we feel has wounded us what happened to us from our perspective, regardless of whether they're receptive to hearing us, have died or are no longer in our lives. Writing a letter as mentioned earlier can be of value, as can bringing them into our meditation time and communicating whatever it is that we need to say to that person then and there. As I have said before, when we want peace more than revenge, more than being right, more than blame, more than anything, the path to forgiveness will come. We don't condone a person's action yet we can forgive the being that committed the action. It can be helpful to understand that everyone is doing the best they know how given who they are, what has happened to them and what they've made of what has happened to them.

Emotional Healing

Edwina rang the Quest for Life Centre after seeing an article in the newspaper about our work. She told the following story to one of our counsellors.

Edwina had nursed her brother, her sister and her husband

through their illnesses and had been present with each of them when they died. She had no remaining family in her age group and had decided that she would never be a burden to her own children and grandchildren.

Edwina was quite well though she had been receiving radiotherapy for advanced breast cancer. She was intending to take her own life in the next few weeks rather than allow herself to get to the stage where she might need nursing herself. Edwina was quite pragmatic in her approach to her life and death but thought she might explore the decision she had come to through one of our programs. We encouraged her to attend a program, as the group environment provides a safe and supportive place in which people can deepen their self-understanding and discover their own best answers. The next program that was appropriate for her to attend was to be held in three weeks' time and the counsellor told Edwina that she'd be sending her a rainbow every day until then.

Edwina participated in the program she attended even though she had to lie down on a day bed for many of the early sessions. She talked frankly about her desire to take her own life rather than see how things might unfold for her. She didn't like the idea of not being in control, nor the idea of inflicting emotional pain on those she loved who would have to care for her if she wasn't to take an active hand in her own demise.

It was during the program, when discussing the side effects of radiotherapy, that Edwina realised she'd been feeling emotionally down and teary for some weeks – a very unusual state for her, as she generally thought people were much better off if they 'just got on with it'. Many people don't realise that one of the side effects for *some* – not all – people having radiotherapy treatment is depression and / or emotional vulnerability. This can start during radiotherapy and may continue for several weeks after its completion.

This information seemed to cheer her somewhat and Edwina agreed that she'd postpone her decision to end her life until after the effects of the radiotherapy had worn off. She also realised that it might be presumptuous to inflict on others the way she'd chosen to deal with emotions herself. After all, how did she know that her family didn't want to care for her if she'd never had the conversation about it with them? Edwina didn't like crying and performed the nursing of her siblings and her husband with efficiency and dedication, but no tears. Edwina realised that in her family of origin they had never talked about feelings and she and her siblings had been encouraged to keep a stiff upper lip in times of adversity. She smiled wryly as I told her that it was very difficult to kiss someone who's keeping a stiff upper lip.

Edwina used the day bed less and less as the week she spent with us progressed and by the end of the program there was a definite twinkle in her eye and a spring in her step. It had been a relief for her to have an environment in which she could explore her thoughts and feelings about life, death, suicide, family, communication and love. Two months later we received a wonderful message from her on our answering machine. 'Hello you lovelies,' she said, 'Thank you for giving me back my life. I'm off for a two-month holiday in Ireland with my son and family. Bye for now.'

Eighteen months later I was delighted to see Edwina's name once again on our participants' list. She was frailer this time but hadn't lost that twinkle or her sense of humour. Edwina used the day bed throughout the program and during the story session told us why she'd returned for another program. Once more she was entertaining the idea of suicide. This time she said she couldn't face the finality of death and losing control of her faculties. The distress it might cause her family no longer worried her as she'd had several conversations with her children since she last had been with us and who, contrary to her presumptions, would find it a privilege to care for her if the need arose.

It was during the practice of *Gift of Forgiveness*, which I mentioned earlier, that Edwina had a realisation about the feelings she was having now. Part of the practice involves seeing ourselves as a child growing through the years and acknowledging the challenges that we might have faced. Edwina saw herself at the age of ten, when she had been hospitalised with a mild form of polio. Because of the partial paralysis, she'd been tied to the bed so that she wouldn't fall out. It had been a distressing and frightening experience for her and she realised that *now* she was afraid of being put in a bed that she'd never get out of because that would be her deathbed. When Edwina was able to shed the tears of the vulnerable and frightened child, she was also able to access the emotion around her present challenge. She wept for her brother, her sister, for her husband and herself, and came to a deep sense of acceptance of the past, present and future.

Our emotional healing lies in the background of our life, waiting for the touch of acknowledgement, acceptance and forgiveness. The last weeks of Edwina's life were filled with laughter, shared memories and tenderness from her children and grandchildren, and she died peacefully at home, surrounded by love, three weeks after she attended our program.

By taking responsibility ('response-ability') for creating the healing of emotional wounds, we find the path to peace. If we avoid taking responsibility for our emotional wounds, peace will surely elude us. The path to peace often goes right through the heart of anguish, despair, anger, frustration, grief or sadness. Our tears become the river of life that carries us to the ocean of peace. The quickest way out is in! One woman described her grief when her husband died in these terms, 'My tears form the river that runs down to my heart.' She liked it when her tears wet her cheeks, ran down her neck and found their way to her chest and heart without the impediment of tissues or mopping up.

Stepping into the unfamiliar territory of emotional healing can be both scary and exciting. Most decent adventures contain these two elements. It's a sure sign that we're on the right track to experiencing the fullness of our own spirit if the journey we're on is a little bit scary and a little bit exciting, especially in the beginning. It's scary because of our mind – held in the personality of the mind / body relationship – and exciting because it comes from our spirit. As we catch sight of our potential and gain confidence in the path, it is no longer scary and simply becomes exciting.

As the emotional wounds of the past are healed, life becomes more and more fulfilling, satisfying and rewarding. The rewards of attending to the healing of our emotions are plentiful and are evidenced by our sense of humour and spontaneity, our creativity and self-confidence. These four aspects are what we sacrifice if we're emotionally weighed down by past traumas that haven't been healed. We lose our sense of humour and spontaneity because we're not here to see what's funny or what there is to respond to; our creativity dries up because creativity is always a present-time activity; and finally, we lose confidence in ourselves or our perception of things.

Stress

A great deal of research has been conducted into whether stress contributes to the development of diseases such as cancer. No amount of research to the contrary would ever convince the tens of thousands of people I've worked with who are certain that stress played a significant part in the cause of their illness.

For many years, these same researching bodies proclaimed that diet had no causal relationship to cancer. Now they've confirmed that diet is implicated in the cause of many cancers – a fact that reason and commonsense would also suggest.

Researchers take major stresses like the loss of a partner, moving house, divorce or long-term unemployment and then measure how many people developed cancer as a consequence of these events.

The premise upon which this kind of research is based seems topsy-turvy to me, as the focus is on the type of stress and how it affects a group of people rather than an individual's reaction to a particular stress. Science resists looking at the individual's reaction and prefers to quantify its findings by focusing only on large groups of people. This is the main limitation of evidence-based medicine – it leaves out the experience of the individual and maintains a simplistic view of disease, health and healing. Not one of us is a group of people. We are each precious individuals and every one of our stories are valid and important.

For one person, moving house might be a sad parting from a lifetime of treasured memories. For another, it might be sheer relief to relocate to a smaller, more manageable space, free of the trappings of the past. Moving house *isn't* the issue. How does a person feel about moving house – *that* is the issue. In fact, I had some clients – Norma and Peter – with precisely this dilemma.

Even though moving house was a mutual decision based on good reasoning, when it came to it, Norma found it very difficult to sort out her possessions and leave her home of many years. It made sense to down-size to a more manageable home and yet, every room of their house was full of her memories. She berated herself over her lack of enthusiasm for the move – telling herself that she should be more mature about it.

Norma's world revolved around her possessions and the stories that belonged to them. They were the outer reference points that connected her to her history and sense of meaning. Their stories gave Norma a framework of connection to events, places and people dear to her. She felt that to relinquish the possessions would be to sacrifice the memories and the meaning in her life.

For Norma's husband, Peter, the story was the opposite. In his early life he'd lost everything he held dear. Through a war he'd lost his home, his business, his country, his first wife and children, and he only treasured the memories in his heart. For Peter, the only things he now treasured were his relationships, so to relinquish possessions was of no consequence for him.

As you might imagine, this proved fertile ground for frustration based on misunderstanding and judgement of one another. Norma wrung her hands as she procrastinated about each decision to forsake a treasure while Peter agitated to pack them up, give them away or throw them out.

For Peter, shifting house was something he welcomed. For Norma, it was the biggest challenge she'd faced in many years and it resulted in her developing insomnia, irritability, anxiety, headaches and digestive problems.

These are many of the common symptoms we might expect to experience when we're not coping well with stress. Most of us have particular ones that we manifest and it's useful to identify which are our favourites. These symptoms are a call for help from our body, mind, emotional world or spirit.

When we're feeling distress, we usually identify a problem as its cause. In Norma's case, she might well have said, 'I'm upset because we're moving.' Yet her reasons for moving were absolutely in agreement with Peter's, which only added to her confusion and distress. We're rarely upset for the reasons we think.

When Norma was able to dissect her feelings about moving she saw that it wasn't the move that was deeply distressing but the relinquishing of most of her prized possessions, under pressure and all at once.

Once she understood her reaction, she felt more compassion and respect for herself. She was already grieving the loss of the community she'd lived in for so long. To have to relinquish her possessions as well, and confront her fears of a future without them, was simply overwhelming.

Berating ourselves only perpetuates the cycle of setting our intention, failing to achieve it and then scolding ourselves for doing so. Once the resistance to feeling the way she did fell away and her self-berating ceased, compassion and understanding entered. Together, Norma and Peter were then able to make new choices. One was to sort out many of her possessions *after* the move and not make the move dependent on when she could bring herself to get rid of them. This released her from the overwhelming feelings of loss and allowed her to deal with them in a more manageable way. It was enough for her to separate from a community she loved, and was much loved by, without adding to it the need for more loss.

Every event is also an opportunity to discover more about ourselves. With compassion and understanding we can see how we forfeit the possibilities of peace in our lives because of our resistance to the way things are. For instance, moving house was something Peter and Norma absolutely agreed was necessary. Moving house became the catalyst by which Norma came to understand and respect herself more deeply. She honoured her way of seeing the world and stopped judging herself just because it was different from Peter's perception. Once more compassionate strategies for this momentous move were evident and exercised, Norma's symptoms of stress disappeared completely.

Peter could have argued that the added cost of transporting possessions that would later be discarded or passed on was crazy – and from his point of view, it was. The frustrations could easily have escalated to all-out war! However, it came down to whether Peter would rather be right or happy. Loving someone implies compassion and understanding for him or her and respect for their foibles.

It is useful to identify the behaviours or activities we engage in when we're not feeling emotionally up to date. Knowing the symptoms of feeling at the end of our tether can be useful when we begin this emotional healing work. Once we identify our favourite physical and emotional reactions to stress we can be on the look-out for them and see their presence as an opportunity to re-establish our priorities. The following list drawn from our Quest for Life Centre programs is not complete in itself. We all have our own particular favourite ways of manifesting stress and some of these reactions may seem repetitive, but each may mean slightly different things to different people.

I would encourage you to write down your favourite half-dozen ways of manifesting stress and stick the piece of paper on your bathroom mirror or somewhere you'll see them regularly. Each day, use this checklist to see how you're feeling about yourself and how you're meeting the challenges in your life. The awareness and recognition of your favourite way of manifesting stress can provide you with inner alarm bells: if you're aware of feeling one or more of these symptoms, respond to the call for help that your body, mind and emotional worlds are giving you.

Common reactions to stress

Walking out of conversations

Irrational fears

Lack of insight into own
  behaviour

Cynicism

Raising our voices

Not breathing

Inability to make decisions

Apathy and inertia

Feeling grouchy and snappy
  and complaining

Hibernating, lying in foetal
  position

Withdrawing sex as a
  punishment

Using inappropriate language

Being negative and sooky

Insomnia or wanting to sleep
  all the time

'Pity partying'

Having sore body parts, where
  everything hurts

Losing perspective

Inability to empathise with
  others

Shortness of breath

Episodes of frenzied housework

Vagueness

Feeling aggro and busy

Feeling trapped or boxed-in

Feeling different from everyone
  else

Martyrdom

Feeling disconnected

Nagging

Shutting down and ignoring
  people

Nausea, queasiness

Beating yourself up with
  shoulds, oughts

Feeling helpless

Craving distractions

Diminished concentration/focus

Impatience/intolerance with people

Blaming

Total apathy

Making rash statements and decisions

Chest pain

Ignoring intuition

Becoming suspicious of self/others

Feeling that your head is going to explode

Planning suicide

Desire to run away

Letting the mad monkey run riot

Having inappropriate conversations

Feeling sick

Feeling unmotivated

Sitting with a glazed look

Listening to sad, loud and torturous music

Feeling numb

Asking, 'Why me???'

Relying on take-away food as your main source of nutrition

Losing your spatial ability

Shut-down of automatic pilot

Adopting pesky behaviours

Self-resentment/hate

Lack of attention when driving

Exhaustion

Decrease in home hygiene standards

Cursing

Loss of perspective

Feeling self-defeated

Rehashing

Loss of skills

Feeling disempowered

Physically throwing things

Rejecting physical contact

Feeling envious

Grinding your teeth

Road rage

Putting yourself in danger

Loss of hope

Saying 'no' to everything

Overspending on credit

Nail-biting

Procrastination

No passion or enthusiasm

Can't plan or see a future

Self-harming behaviours

Argumentative

Choosing negative company

Decrease in personal hygiene standards

Camping out by the fridge

Overeating

Skin disorders/rashes

Constipation

Feeling like you're 'stuck in mud'

Wearing pyjamas all day

Lack of appetite

Recurrent respiratory illnesses

Diarrhoea (dire rear!)

Headaches/migraines

Indigestion

No libido

Herpes/cold sores

Clumsiness

Forgetfulness

Irritability

Short-temperedness

Emotional flatness

Tearful, can't stop crying

Uncommunicative

Experiencing non-stop internal dialogue

Hating yourself

Craving junk foods/sweet things

Palpitations, twitches

Allergies

Increased need for sex (not intimacy)

Hair loss

Restlessness

Absentmindedness

Reactiveness

Engaging in isolating behaviours

Depression

Withdrawal

Confusion

Self-doubt

Mindlessness

Sulkiness or moodiness

Inappropriate retail therapy

Descending into overwhelming sadness

Being prescriptive and controlling

Anxiety or panic attacks

Adopting addictive or compulsive behaviours, including drugs, eating, smoking, gambling, drinking alcohol, shopping, sex, chocolate, coffee in *excess*.

Do any of these behaviours or disorders appear in your life? These are the symptoms of *not being in the present*; when we're emotionally weighed down by the past and our feelings are not acknowledged or up to date. Their presence can be helpful warning signs that something has gone amiss and we need to reassert our commitment to emotional healing.

Such symptoms of being overwhelmed by life are not just a range of behaviours related to a state of mind. They also reflect a state of physiology within our body. We secrete the chemicals of powerlessness, being overwhelmed, panic and despair and they have significant consequences in our physical health.

Nourishing the Spirit Within

It is equally important for us to know the things that nourish, replenish and reconnect us to our spirit; that nourish, replenish and 'fluff up' our body; that inspire, uplift, nourish and quieten our mind. In what way do we give healthy expression to our emotions? In what environments do we feel connected to our spirit?

This list, too, will be very individual but might contain some common answers to the questions above. I encourage you to write down your half-dozen ways of replenishing yourself on all levels and likewise put that list where you'll see it every day. Make sure you include something from your list in your life each day.

I nourish my physical, mental, emotional and spiritual self by

Perfumes that delight

Massage

Spas

Long walks along the beach

Dancing

Listening to music

Inspirational reading, poetry

Loving someone

Pursuing a creative outlet

Listening to the radio

Achieving goals

Drives in the country

Making love and enjoying intimacy

Using aromatherapy

Taking bubble baths by candlelight

Being in nature

Singing

Making music

Meditation

Buying myself something special

Learning or studying something new

Strategy and planning

Kissing, cuddling

Giving love to family

Being silly with/without kids

Dressing up

Going to the theatre

Contact with good friends

Enjoying my work

Doing things for other people

Prayer

Laughter

Visiting gardens and gardening

Sport and exercise

Going on picnics

Good communication

Contemplation

Painting

Keeping a diary

Having a good cry

Keeping a blessing book

Spending time with my pets

Having times of solitude

Writing a journal, poetry

Drawing and sketching

Yoga, tai chi, chi gong

Spending special time with
 special people

Changing my bed sheets

Taking holidays

Buying flowers for myself

Volunteering

Hugging trees

Walking barefoot on grass

Giving someone a compliment

Sitting and relaxing

Permitting myself to have 'down'
 time

Giving someone a massage

Keeping to a routine

Spiritual practices or rituals

Eating a healthy diet and
 drinking juices

Craftwork or hobbies

Curling up with a book

Staring into the distance

Sitting in starlight, firelight,
 candlelight

Seeing funny movies

Being in the company of children
 and animals

It also seems that most men need to spend time in a 'shed', either real or metaphorical.

These are all present-time activities. We love being in the present. With these activities we're not preoccupied with the future or the past. What stops us from having a life that is full of these activities? Some people blame time yet we know there are 168 hours in the week and every one of them belongs to us. Some people feel guilty or selfish having these things abundantly in their life, yet the greatest gift we can give ourselves, our children, our community or the planet is the gift of our own excellent physical, mental, emotional and spiritual health.

When we give these things or activities a priority in our life we will rarely venture to our list of stress symptoms. It is our responsibility to refill our 'inner bucket' until it is full to overflowing – then we can give from the overflow in our life. No-one else can fill our bucket for us; it's our responsibility. If we're always giving from a half-empty bucket then we resent what we have to give to others that we haven't even given to ourselves.

Seeking Support

Many people benefit from having validation and guidance as they undertake this journey of creating peace in their lives. Some people might find the support of their close friends and family is sufficient. However, most of us benefit from the more skilled and objective help a therapist, counsellor, teacher or support group provides.

Some people are reticent about seeking assistance, believing it to be a sign of weakness. They often wait until a crisis happens in their life before they seek this sort of help. Many of the people who attend my Quest for Life Centre programs are faced with their mortality through the advent of serious illness. This confrontation with mortality brings into focus the lack of balance and peace in a person's life. It is this that precipitates their journey into deeper healing and it is a joy to work with them because their commitment to peace is at the forefront of their minds and hearts, and they're willing to embrace this healing *now*.

For others, grief or loss, anxiety, depression or loss of meaning or identity has been the cause of their attendance at some sort of program. Others come because they can no longer continue their life with the inner turmoil left in the wake of sexual, emotional or physical abuse in their childhood. More and more people now attend programs because they want a more meaningful and satisfying life that is congruent with their values and aspirations.

It can be a challenge to find a good support group, counsellor, teacher or therapist. Speak to friends who share your interests and ask if they know of someone or a group in your area. Any good counsellor, group, teacher or therapist will always empower you to have confidence and trust in your own self. You are the world authority on you. No-one knows you better than you do. The mark of a good therapist is that you leave their company feeling better about yourself and your ability to deal with life's challenges.

I guarantee that once you commit yourself to inner healing, the whole universe will conspire to bring it about and you will find the stepping stones to your own spirit. You will find that people, books, tapes, lectures, articles and more will come your way and that you only need a willingness to heal to set this process in motion.

By all means, gain the assistance of meditation, a counsellor, a course, keep a journal, attend a group or read books about this inner journey. You do not have to earn your emotional healing or do it on your own. Indeed, I have found that meditation, counselling and / or group work dramatically speed up the process of our own self-understanding and discovery.

If you need to, shriek it to the universe – demand that your intuition be present and guide you to the experience of your own essential nature. Nature abhors a vacuum and if your desire for peace is strong, it will surely come. The path to peace may present itself in unexpected ways so you might need to remind yourself that 'nothing wrong is happening' – all things are unfolding for this purpose. Experiencing this profound peace that is beyond all understanding is the only reason you are alive and breathing.

When the revelation of our consciousness is our goal then every moment becomes an opportunity to experience it or release our resistance to 'what is'. Suddenly we see life winking at us everywhere.

No-one can fix you, change you or make you better. You are perfect just as you are. Experiencing your own dear self – the source of joys, sorrows, fears, vulnerabilities and more – you discover the essential self, your spirit, your consciousness; the vastness that feels all, yet clings to nothing and nothing clings to it. In this vastness of consciousness there is only love, only joy, only unity.

Awareness provides the understanding of how our thoughts, feelings and beliefs influence our lives. When we come to this realisation we empower ourselves to deal creatively with the many challenging situations that life presents us. We are no longer victims of our circumstances. We are active participants in the events of our life.

Your value lies not in what you *do* in the world; it lies in who you 'be' – we are human beings rather than human doings. *You* are the gift. You deliver the gift of yourself through your doing. Our value lies in the depth and knowledge of our consciousness, not in the outer circumstances of our lives.

Your life matters enough to take an active role in how you perceive the world, others and yourself. Everything in the universe is in flux. The planet is in motion; nature is in motion. Everything we perceive is in motion. Nothing is fixed. Once you hear the voice of your spirit calling you to consciousness, all of life's experiences take on a new meaning. You notice that there are no coincidences; that every encounter is a sacred encounter; that every moment is a sacred moment. In this way your life becomes sacred, feels sacred, is sacred. Living your life from the inside out, from this sacred perspective, not waiting for the world to change, you become the change you wish to see and experience the power of pure consciousness that permeates yourself and the universe in which you live.

The Petrea King Quest for Life Centre

At the Petrea King Quest for Life Centre, we give people practical strategies for living well in challenging circumstances and for finding meaning in the midst of life's unexpected events. We recognise that we can't always change what happens to us in life but we can play an active role in how we're going to respond to what happens to us. We value peace of mind above all else.

There are many events in life that stop us in our tracks and cause us to consider how best to meet the challenges we face: an unexpected diagnosis, an accident, loss or tragedy can be such an impetus.

Some people seek more meaningful ways of managing the challenging circumstances of chronic illness, multiple loss, anxiety, relationship breakdown, depression or the consequences of past abuse. Other people choose to take time-out to review their life with the intention of deepening their relationship with themselves and living a more satisfying and meaningful life in the future.

Since 1985 more than 50,000 people have attended residential programs or counselling with me and my team of trained health professionals.

Since 1999 our residential programs and services have been conducted at the Quest for Life Centre – an historic guesthouse set in 3.6 tranquil hectares of gardens at Bundanoon, in the beautiful Southern Highlands of New South Wales.

Our programs endeavour to support each participant to regain a sense of control over their lives and actively participate in their own healing. Each person leaves with a greater understanding of themselves and a deeper respect for their unique story. Content of the programs is tailored to the people attending and varies accordingly. Programs include the following five areas:

Techniques for living in the present

- Relaxation, visualisation and meditation techniques

- Living the life you came here to live

- Transforming adversity; learning to respond, not react

Mind–body connection

- The science of stress and illness

- Creating an environment for healing

- Harnessing the power of the mind

- The role of intuition

Managing thoughts and emotions

- Peace of mind: what it is and how to attain and maintain it

- Understanding the power of the mind to create and counter stress

- Forgiveness and getting 'up to date'

- What is a positive attitude; how to attain and maintain it

Complementary advice supporting medical treatment

- Natural therapies to help with pain, sleep, symptoms and side effects

- Practical advice on diet

Moving on from here

- Rearranging priorities

- Enhancing communication, resilience, relationships

- Getting back in the driver's seat of life

- Learning to live skilfully with stress and move beyond difficult emotions

If you feel we can assist you through one of our residential programs or other services, please call us with your particular needs. We look forward to our paths crossing with yours.

The Quest for Life Foundation

The Petrea King Quest for Life Centre is owned and operated by the Quest for Life Foundation, a registered charity established in 1990 by Petrea King.

The Quest for Life Foundation subsidises all programs as well as an additional subsidy with the support of the NSW Health Department for people on pensions and low incomes.

Donations assist us to support the provision and expansion of our services and are fully tax deductible.

Petrea King Quest for Life Centre
PO Box 390
Bundanoon NSW 2578
Australia
Ph: (61 2) 4883 6599
Fax: (61 2) 4883 6755
Email: info@questforlife.com.au
Web: www.questforlife.com.au

Petrea King Collection

Much of life is spent taking on more information, more identities and more learning. We then identify who we are by what we do. In meditation we unveil the treasure of our human 'being' beyond our human 'doing'.

As we quieten the chatter of our minds we discover an inner wellspring from which intuition, joy, inspiration, imagination, wisdom and contentment more effortlessly flow. Meditation becomes that sacred space in which we replenish and refresh ourselves.

Your life matters. You are not here by chance. You are here to make the journey of your life by taking responsibility for your physical, mental, emotional and spiritual wellbeing. My books and meditation practices detail practical ways in which you can reclaim your life and establish peace of mind. I trust they will assist you in creating health, happiness and harmony in your life.

Relaxation and Meditation Practices available on CD

Learning to Meditate

This title combines an excellent explanation of meditation with a guided progressive relaxation and meditation practice with Petrea.

You will learn what meditation is and how to practise it. You will understand when and why to practise meditation, how the mind works and how to manage it more effectively.

Sleep (formerly Sleep Easy)

No-one has ever heard the end of this practice! Designed to guide you into deep and restful sleep, it is ideal for the chronic insomniac or people having temporary difficulty with sleeping. You are guided through a progressive relaxation then into a beautiful garden of peace where sleep will overtake you. The CD comes with a bonus booklet of tips from Petrea for developing good sleep habits.

Relaxation

A guided relaxation to release stress and increase immune function. We imagine we're at the beach, where we put all our stresses in a rainbow hot air balloon and release it. We enter the water and, floating on our back, bathe in the golden light of the sun and feel its healing energy. After a brief meditation we return refreshed and energised. Plus the relaxing silver flute music of Gopal.

Golden Light Meditation

Petrea guides you through a progressive relaxation and uses golden light imagery through the body to create a powerful environment for physical, emotional and spiritual healing. After a brief meditation we return refreshed and energised. Plus the beautiful healing music of Windsong by Phil Colville.

Increasing Self Esteem

Petrea talks about what makes or damages self-esteem and how we can improve our self-confidence. We are guided deep into the rainforest where there's a waterfall cascading into a peaceful pool of water and visualise ourselves living with all the qualities we want in our life. This practice is helpful in changing negative attitudes or for goal-setting and is a favourite with teenagers and adults.

Gift of Forgiveness

Through extending compassionate self-forgiveness we can enter a deeper relationship with ourselves and others built on self-understanding. In these two practices Petrea guides you through a progressive relaxation, then using imagery to connect with the qualities of our inner child we extend forgiveness to ourselves and others.

Rainbows to Heal

Petrea guides you through a progressive relaxation and self-healing practice that uses imagery to fill your energy centres with the colours of the rainbow. A second practice involves extending the colours of the rainbow to bring love or healing to another person or situation.

Healing Journey

Petrea guides you through a progressive relaxation and into a beautiful garden where water and light bring about peace and healing. After a brief meditation we return refreshed and energised. This is an ideal practice for those who want to create wellness, inner peace, strength and self-confidence. Plus the beautiful healing music of *Windsong* by Phil Colville.

Dolphin Magic

Journey deep beneath the sea with your own special dolphin to a crystal cavern full of the colours of the rainbow. Allow the colours to wash through your body to bring feelings of peace and renewal. After a healing meditation you return to the surface with your dolphin, refreshed and energised. Plus the beautiful healing music of *Earthsea* by Phil Colville.

Soar Like an Eagle

High on a mountaintop at sunset you relax and enjoy the peace and serenity before floating effortlessly as an eagle. Entering a meditation you absorb the qualities of self-confidence, strength, wisdom and clarity and return refreshed and energised. Plus the beautiful healing music of Solis by Phil Colville.

Zen Garden

A beautiful relaxation and meditation practice set in a garden full of cherry blossoms. We meet our wise inner being by a pool of water and ask for the gift of a quality we need or the answer to a question. We return refreshed and energised, bringing back with us what we need. Plus the beautiful silver flute music of Gopal.

Releasing Pain

Using progressive relaxation and imagery to release physical, mental and emotional pain, Petrea guides you through a relaxation and the practice of Yoga Nidra to effectively manage and release pain.

Books by Petrea

Sometimes Hearts Have to Break: 25 Inspirational Stories of Healing and Peace

Sometimes Hearts Have to Break details Petrea's story and those of 25 people whose lives she has enriched and been enriched by in return. These stories are full of hope – for the future, for healing, for finding peace, for reconciliation with the past. The people in this book are a tribute to the human spirit. The events of our lives, however tragic, can be a catalyst by which we shed all that stands in the way of feeling deeply alive and at peace.

Spirited Women: Journeys with Breast Cancer

Spirited Women addresses the many practical issues women face when diagnosed with breast cancer. The book has quotes from hundreds of women who describe their diverse reactions to things such as diagnosis, choosing doctors, confronting their scars, sexuality and body image, talking to children, living with uncertainty, dealing with recurrence, facing death, letting go, resolving the past and learning to live more abundantly and peacefully in the present. In addition, there is a wealth of practical information that educates and empowers those whose lives are touched by breast cancer.

Quest for Life: Living Well with Cancer and Life-threatening Illnesses

This bestseller is an essential handbook for anyone with cancer and for those who love or care for them. It is the story of Petrea's recovery from leukaemia combined with the practical knowledge gained from working with tens of thousands of individuals with cancer and other life-challenging illnesses.

In *Quest for Life* Petrea provides accessible guidelines for combining the best of medical care with commonsense lifestyle practices and naturopathic advice – all based on Petrea's training in health, healing and meditation.

For further information or orders, please contact:

Petrea King
PO Box 190
Bundanoon NSW 2578
Australia
Ph: (61 2) 4883 6805
Fax: (61 2) 4883 6632
Email: info@petreaking.com
Web: www.petreaking.com